SEARCHING EVERYWHERE FOR GOD

A spiritual exploration for scientific times

by

JULIA HOLLAND

The searching and misadventures of a lifetime reveal insights that make ancient wisdom relevant to all of us

Praise for *Searching Everywhere for God*

"An excellent read, not only as a beautiful reflection of one woman's journey to enlightenment, but as part of a larger effort towards establishing scientific and spiritual reconciliation. The reflections, lessons and perspectives shared in this book are both thought provoking and enlightening, such that I found myself very much at peace within the pages, absolutely glued to the end. Beautifully written."

Sean Wade-McCue, PhD Candidate and Engineer within Artificial Intelligence and Robotics

"Julia beautifully and skilfully weaves the complex threads of personal life experience, with the equally alive, vibrant and rigorous inquiry (and research) into its true meaning – all infused with her astute clarity and direct insight."

Mardi Fielding, Yoga Teacher

"Julia Holland's breathtaking personal narrative drives us along jungle paths, roads, highways and into space in search of that one unifying experience of Self Awareness. From Shankara to Osho, Ramana to Bohm it is at once a familiar road and an exquisite dance between the mystic and the mortgage; the everyday and the infinite. Many have walked it; Julia has written it down."

John Maynard, Archive Consultant to Ramanasramam (Volunteer)

"Julia Holland's book provides a much needed antidote to the polarity of the debate between those people who feel that science is the final authority in understanding our place in the universe, and those people who reject science because science seems to reject the idea of God or of there being a creative intelligence behind the physical manifestation of the universe. Her book, partly by going into her personal experience, and partly through an examination of what others have thought and discovered, investigates what it means to be conscious and what it means to believe in the existence of a personal self. Instead of arguing about ideas, the book is concerned with the possibility of a direct experience of what lies behind our notions of separateness and individuality."

Dr John Thornton, Honorary Reader and Teaching Fellow, School of Engineering and Informatics, University of Sussex
Adjunct Associate Professor, Institute for Integrated and Intelligent Systems, Griffith University

Cover concept: Abi Stephenson
Cover design: John Wade
Editor: Wendy Yorke

ISBN 978-0-9570722-8-2

Literary Agent: Wendy Yorke
WRITE. EDIT. PUBLISH
www.wendyyorke.com

Published by Shimran
an imprint of Fitzrovia Press
Glastonbury BA6 8HF, UK
www.fitzroviapress.co.uk

text FSC white bookwove 80gsm vol 17.5
cover 260gsm one-sided board
text set in Centaur 13 pt on 16 pt

Printed and bound in Great Britain
by Grosvenor Group Print Services Ltd
Essex IG10 3TS

"I have repeatedly said that in my opinion the idea of a personal God is a childlike one. You may call me an agnostic, but I do not share the crusading spirit of the professional atheist whose fervour is mostly due to a painful act of liberation from the fetters of religious indoctrination received in youth. I prefer an attitude of humility corresponding to the weakness of our intellectual understanding of nature and of our own being."

Albert Einstein

About the Author

Julia Holland has made a lifelong exploration—both practical and theoretical—of the search for meaning and 'God'.

Her quest has taken her to the feet of many masters from Krishnamurti to Rajneesh, from Australian guru Barry Long to Ramesh Balsekar. She has also explored the interface of science and religion, including contemporary scientific ideas on the origins of the universe, quantum physics, consciousness and the nature of the self.

In between living a 'normal life' as mother and writer, she has often visited India.

Julia's credentials are not as a philosophy academic or as any sort of minister of religion but as an ordinary human being who has searched for God and found a taste of truth through direct experience. This is the traditional mystical path beyond logic but she is keen to take on the difficult task of trying to communicate logically what is beyond definition, drawing on many sources that reflect her experience.

Julia's 'day job' has prepared her for this through a long career in copywriting and business communication. She has also had four young-adult fiction books published.

Julia was born in England, moved to Australia in 1990 and now lives in Brisbane, Australia.

DEDICATION

To all those friends who have shared my search,
and for my daughter and her father who suffered most
because of my restless quest for something I couldn't find
at that time in settled family life.

CONTENTS

Praise for *Searching Everywhere for God* ii
About the Author vi
Map of India xi
Introduction 1
Prelude in Singapore 5

Part One A PERSONAL JOURNEY

1 What to believe? 11
2 India beckons 21
3 Cult or spiritual commune? 36
4 Commitment, confusion, commitment... 47
5 Beginnings and endings 59
6 World turned upside down 69
7 The end of my tether 82
8 A surprise glimpse 91

Part Two EXPLORING NON-DUALITY

9	Living without myself	101
10	Beyond the filter of self	111
11	The heart of it all	121
12	What about God?	134
13	A creator God?	143
14	Masters of non-duality	154
15	The pain and purpose of separation	166
16	The dilemma of the decision-maker	179

Part Three SPIRITUALITY FOR THE FUTURE

17	The fight for our souls	193
18	Quantum physics beside the temple	204
19	Oneness in diversity	213
20	Religion without frontiers	221
21	Back to the source	232

Epilogue	241
Explanation of Indian/Sanskrit terms	247
BIBLIOGRAPHY	250
References	255

INDIAN JOURNEYS 1977-2013
1977 Amritsar › Pune › Agra › Varanasi › Kathmandu
1979 Mumbai › Pune
1981 › Mumbai › Pune › Mahabaleshwar
2004 Chennai › Mahabalipuram › Tiruvanamalai › Pondicherry ✈ Mumbai › Nasik
2007-8 Mumbai ✈ Chennai › Chidambaram
2012-13 Kochi › Kozhikode › Mysore › Coimbatore › Madurai › Tirucharappalli › Tiruvanamalai › Chennai ✈ Varanasi › Allahabad
Amritsar
NEPAL
NEW DELHI
Agra
Kathmandu
RAJASTHAN
Allahabad
Varanasi
Nasik
MUMBAI
Pune
Mahabaleshwar
CHENNAI
Tiruvanamalai
Mahabalipuram
Mysore
Pondicherry
Tirucharapalli
Chidambaram
Coimbatore
Kochi
Madurai

INTRODUCTION

Over recent generations, science has cut the religious ground from under our feet and asking us to believe in God is like asking us to believe that the world is flat.

With the overload of information and secular concerns, it has become increasingly hard for the everyday man or woman to know what to believe and often there is a vacuum of meaninglessness where religion used to be a guiding beacon.

Can an ordinary, non-aligned person have something of significance to add to this debate? I believe we can and must.

The voices we hear are usually either those of scientists with a narrow, specialised focus—and often a strong atheist agenda—or they are of the ministers or theologians of specific religions who also have a vested interest and an important power-base to protect. Sometimes we hear from a journalist or a naive seeker who does a quick tour of religious thought (often in India) as an outsider looking in and becomes an instant expert. Recently we've also heard from professional philosophers and humanists who believe we can have the 'good bits' of religion without the awkward God bits.

Few of those with the loudest voices acknowledge that what we seek may be, by its very nature, beyond mental activity; that it is ultimately something to experience, not something that can be reached by discussion, logic or analysis.

I have attempted the almost impossible task of drawing together the threads of mysticism and science through sharing my own search for some transcendent truth that lies beneath or beyond everything. It is a journey of at least 50 years along obscure tracks twisting across continents and through the challenges of everyday life.

On one side, it has led me to the inevitable experiences of sitting on hard floors in awkward postures getting bitten by mosquitoes and trying to be beyond thought—my periodic efforts pretty feeble compared with those who endure austerities for years—and going humbly to the feet of various bearded gurus who claim to have worthwhile knowledge. On the other side, it has been about integrating hard-won glimpses of insight with the latest discoveries of science to try to develop a coherent big picture that satisfies the doubting mind.

All of this hasn't resulted in a book of the 'How to improve yourself and find God in a weekend' genre but I hope it will reveal valuable perspectives that have emerged as some of the scattered jigsaw pieces have fallen into place for me.

It is not so much an 'Eat Pray Love' experience but more a 'Search Stumble Question' experience—with love making a few appearances along the way!

The names of people in this book have been changed to protect their privacy.

PRELUDE IN SINGAPORE

I GUESS MOST OF US periodically review our lives and try to put some meaning or story around the things that have unfolded. For me there is a natural period of reassessment with the recent death of my father and with my 60th birthday not too far over the horizon. A modest inheritance gives me the chance to take a few months off work to try to draw many threads together into a coherent fabric. While we may all try to make sense of our experience and fit it to a narrative, this journey is particularly focused on what I have learned about 'the big questions' that have pre-occupied me since a young age and which have driven me on a lifelong search of philosophy, science and religion—while keeping one foot in touch with the solid land of real-world job, motherhood and mortgage.

Have I learnt anything? What have multiple meditations, gurus and books led me to? What can I say I really know that is deeper than the nice aphorisms that get passed around in well-meaning circles and on Facebook? How can I reconcile the brief periods of unquestionable knowing with the reality of science that says they are all too questionable? Has the search been worth the sacrifices it has often demanded? While this is very much a personal journey, I believe it also reflects the questions we all face in trying to find some truth or purpose that grounds our life in more than materialistic acquisition and individual achievement. I'm on my way to India again because India is my default place for reflection and to step outside the wall-to-wall demands of daily life. In India you can't help but shake free of the deadening grasp of routine and face life in all its raw craziness, pain and joy.

Thirty years ago, I went to India driven by a desperate need to understand life and find meaning. Now, after pursuing that quest along an unpredictable and sometimes rocky path, I am returning to sift through the significance and insignificance of the many steps along the way. I've made a stopover in Singapore to break my flight from Australia and, before the muted tropical dawn spills through the humid streets, I walk to the Sri Veeramakaliamman Temple in Little India.

I leave my sandals at the temple door and touch the worn stone step beneath the arched entrance. Then I make my way through the milling crowds as inconspicuously as possible to sit in front of a larger-than-life but very lifelike statue of goddess Durga. She is clad in more gold and finery than a starlet at the Oscars with her multiple arms holding symbolic objects that link her to other manifestations of the goddess and to the myths that tell stories of her power. She's the one that a friend of mine referred to as 'the original multi-tasking woman'!

The *brahmin* priest adjusts her huge golden mayoral-like chain so it sits flat across her left breast and offers a silver tray with a flaming lamp above his head. A wide range of Indians comes for the blessings, holding hands to the flame and touching their chests, before marking their foreheads with red *kum kum* powder. There are sari-clad women, younger women in jeans and fashions tops, an older man in faded and well-worn pants and shirt, a middle-aged man in smart shirt and business pants. One of the younger women leaves orchids as an offering. A trendier young man in black t-shirt and camouflage pants hangs back and takes a photo of Durga on his mobile phone.

I sense the reverence and meaning invested in this place and silently ask for blessings on this venture before holding my own hands to the flame, which is now unattended on the table in front of the goddess. It's a simple request and a gesture that encapsulates the faith and hope integral to the simplest spiritual practice. While I don't believe in a personal god or goddess sitting waiting to heed my prayers, there is something meaningful about acknowledging my individual insignificance and powerlessness against the much larger movements of life and death. I am happy to be part of this incredible dance of humanity and to bow down to something transcendent, however intangible and illogical it may seem.

I know it is the same impulse that moves all those with a spiritual dimension to their lives, if that dimension is not simply an empty ritual or social convenience. Whether it is a Catholic lighting a candle in front of the Virgin Mary or a Muslim bowing to Mecca, or a Buddhist spinning a prayer wheel, there is a deep sense of aligning one's life to something greater through the devotion or surrender of the individual. This is much more than the scientific and objective observer might gauge from watching the scene, when it can easily be interpreted as sending a naive shopping list to 'an imaginary friend' or storing up a good scoresheet for the afterlife—a psychological need for those who are weak or powerless. While there are inevitably people who relate to their religion in this way and, while it doubtless plays an important role of comforter to millions, to dismiss all religion as this seems to me to miss the greater and deeper part of it.

PART ONE

A PERSONAL JOURNEY

I

WHAT TO BELIEVE?

MY BIG QUESTIONS started long before my first trip to India—in a small convent classroom in a small town in England. My first memory of pondering what life was all about was while reading the little red Catholic catechism we learnt by rote at six or seven years old.

> *Q: Who made me?*
> *A: God made me.*
> *Q: Why did God make me?*
> *A: God made me to know him and love him and serve him in this world and be happy with him forever in the next.*

In the way of 1950s Roman Catholic education, I was offered the sense of being in God's chosen religion—unlike the second-class Church of England, which was wicked Henry VIII's breakaway group with no direct authority via the Pope from God! I had, by good fortune, been baptised but had a duty to stand up for God even unto death. Martyrs were not only inspiration from the past. We could also be called on to be martyrs if the communists burst into our classroom and demanded we stamp on the crucifix—at that age I had little sense of how likely that scenario was and worried whether I would have the fidelity and courage expected of me.

Another weighty duty was to baptise any un-baptised babies that were in danger of death. Citizens could undertake a baptism ceremony in this circumstance to save a baby being sent to Limbo for eternity where it would never see God. Even at primary school age, I felt a strong sense of injustice for all those babies who, through no fault of their own, would languish in a no man's land forever. At least saving one would only require facing a reluctant parent, not a communist with a gun!

There was a line of dialogue opened up with God—largely a one-way request line with prayers for good weather for the school fete, to bless my family or to help with passing school tests. But occasionally I talked to God to share my questions or uncertainty—and hoped he was listening.

There were also the young rites of passage of first confession and first communion, heavy with significance for a Catholic child. First communion was the most memorable with its white dress and veil, sweet-smelling orange blossom in my hair-band, and the gift of a little white missal with coloured pictures amongst the text. Confirmation was a year or two later and it felt a more serious and responsible occasion—the bishop was coming and he definitely got a big build-up as a living legend of holiness.

Behind the preparation for celebration milestones, school was also a threatening environment for me. The old-style convent meals—over-boiled potatoes, baked beans and luncheon meat or gristly mince—wouldn't go down. I gagged and toyed with the items on my plate, trying to make it look as if I'd eaten something. Sister Francis, the headmistress, tried to force-feed me once or twice but settled for a 'no eat, no play' policy.

Many days I sat alone on a hard chair in the classroom, eyes closed, listening to the sound of children playing outside. Although I didn't know it, this may have been my first taste of meditation.

I also developed bad headaches, particularly on Monday when the worst meal had to be faced. By the time I got home I had to retreat to bed. My grandmother—who also suffered from headaches—brought a facecloth soaked in 4711 eau-de-cologne to drape over my forehead. Again, I closed my eyes and listened to sounds, not thinking too much, only aware of the pain and the distant hub-bub of family life.

There was the famous Catholic guilt too. I knew many of the things I did were hurting Jesus and, by the age of eight or nine, I had committed a mortal sin by taking communion after breaching the required fasting period beforehand. This worried me. I tried to imagine what hell would feel like. Death became a worry. 'Eternity' was a concept I tried to get my mind around and the idea of burning for eternity cast a shadow over my enjoyment of life for quite some time.

Catholicism from my mother's side of the family was balanced by a father who questioned the facts I brought home from school. "So, you think the world is only 4000 years old?" he'd challenge over the dinner table. He also threw strange stories into the mix that were intriguing but never presented as doctrine. They were often presaged by 'They say'. "They say there are men in the Himalayas who can sit naked in the snow by increasing their own body heat."

Given a choice of high schools, I rejected the convent option and went to a state grammar school. There I had to sit out the standard scripture lessons in the library, stay late on Fridays for a special Catholic session and go to the local priest on Saturday mornings for further instruction. The Catholics weren't about to let go of me and there was great fear then that the purity of Catholic thought would be contaminated even by other Christian perspectives.

Despite their best intentions, they couldn't protect me from the doubts in my own mind.

The dilemma facing me at 14 years old was much the same dilemma facing many of us in society today. We would really like to believe in God or an intelligence behind the universe but we look for proof and find it very hard to come by.

When I tackled this conundrum with all the intensity and rebelliousness of my teenage years, my Catholic priest tried to reclaim me to the fold by explaining the merits of 'faith'. I couldn't see how one could force oneself to dispel doubts. I felt that I needed to *experience* God in some way. Simply believing because a priest said so struck me as very shaky ground. How could I know that this was the right belief when other people in the world believed different things? How could I build a view of the world and a way of life around a belief system that might crumble in the reality of death?

Behind the doubt, there was also a certainty that, if there was a great and wise God, he would surely not have the narrow-minded approach that only people from a certain religion would be saved. Surely good motivations and kindness to others would be recognised by God, regardless of whether the person was Catholic, Church of England, Hindu, Buddhist or Muslim. Or even if that person was someone who had escaped the march of missionaries and had never heard of any of these religions.

Then there was the problem of Jesus. At that stage, I had enough connection with the religion of my childhood to spend one day during the Easter school holiday moving around the church, kneeling for 5-10 minutes at each of the 'Stations of the Cross' and contemplating the gruelling scenes of Jesus' trial and crucifixion. I felt deeply touched by his suffering and in awe of his endurance. I related to him as a great and courageous man; a human being who felt the pain I could feel. But was he really God's only son? Could the Immaculate Conception really be true? And what was wrong with conceiving in the good-old fashioned way, which presumably God had provided, if he existed?

The resurrection was another challenge to credulity. As Father Christmas, the tooth-fairy and other sources of magic had been debunked, it was natural to question whether one could really believe in someone rising from the dead. My rational mind felt that, if there had been a historical Jesus, he probably hadn't been completely dead after the crucifixion. To trump the resurrection, there was his bodily ascension into heaven forty days later. Such unaided space travel seemed unlikely to me even then.

In more recent years, one of the most telling comments on the clash between science and traditional belief was the assertion that, if Jesus had ascended towards the sky in around 33 CE and travelled at the speed of light, he still wouldn't be beyond the Milky Way. Presumably he would need some sort of listening device to pick up all of our prayers on the way too.

In every religious tradition, the gods, saints and prophets are associated with miracles or activity outside normal material reality. The Catholic Church still canonises saints on the basis of three proven miracles. It is this miraculous intervention we really yearn for as a sign to be convinced that there is more to life than solid matter and as proof that the person we revere is someone special beyond normal humanity. I've heard it often in India too—in fact, much more often in India. There, the boundaries of belief are still more flexible for most people and there is a long tradition of holy men who can appear in two places at one time, foretell someone's arrival, know someone's inner secrets, grant people's wishes or heal their woes.

My Indian guide at the 2013 Kumbh Mela festival and his friend, a respected surgeon in Western medicine, spoke openly about miracles, such as mango trees bearing fruit out of season in the ashram of a holy woman. They even spoke of a holy saint who had died and migrated to a disciple's body where he continued to teach.

This belief in the miraculous is also shared by many in the New Age movement. There are hundreds of books selling the message that we only need to believe in something or think positively to make a wish reality. Although there is certainly evidence that the mind can affect the body, and a positive attitude tends to open doors, I don't think we can manipulate matter that easily. I often think of the displaced refugees or people in extreme poverty and wonder if the New Age prophets are implying that all such people need is a few affirmations and they too could instantly rise above their situation and have a life of abundance.

As science perceives everything in a logical, materialistic framework, and religious believers mix wishful thinking with the intuitive sense that there is more than mechanistic matter, it's no wonder we get into impossibly polarised arguments with religion and science on opposite sides of the table.

For me in my teen years, these polarities were coming into focus but the world was still largely unexplored and I had no real sense of what was possible.

I knew I couldn't blindly believe but I was hungry for glimpses of something that that might underlie or interpenetrate the material world.

I had high expectations when the school invited some 'alternative religions' to speak to us—and somehow I slipped through the Catholic segregation net to be allowed to attend these. I remember a woman from the Quakers talking about speaking in tongues, which seemed to confirm the Pentecostal story from the New Testament, and someone from Christian Scientists who gave us a long history of their religion.

I was most excited when someone was coming to demonstrate meditation as I felt that might really be a doorway to actually experiencing things differently. The young woman put an apple on the desk and talked to us about meditating on the apple. "Think of nothing but the apple," she said. "Think about its skin, think about its flesh, think about its core, think about its seeds, think about the smell of it and the taste of it, think about the tree where it grew and how that tree grew…"

I did my best to explore the apple conceptually from every angle but it was a very boring half hour with no results. Annoyance and disappointment mingled. If that was meditation, I didn't see what it had to offer me.

I left high school with the big questions unanswered and an underlying desire to know for sure if God existed and if there were really miracles—and why we were here at all. As there were no promising avenues to explore for answers, the questions had to go on the back burner for now.

I'd already given up going to mass and become a fairly rebellious teenager, sometimes skipping school with my friend Lesley to wander off for the day, sharing cigarettes as we talked. At other times, I was to be found washing up in the local bikers' café or speeding across the countryside on the back of a motorbike. Now I shed my school uniform, flared my jeans with floral inserts and plunged into my generation's quest for love, harmony and good music.

The next glimmer of possibility in my quest was at age

16 when, loitering awkwardly by the coffee vending machine at college, I met a fellow student named John. He was a tall young man with a gentle voice who seemed to share some of my introspective leanings and intense questioning of life. We had many earnest discussions in cafes and pubs, and I borrowed his *Psychic News,* which had incredible tales of spirits of the dead returning to give messages through mediums or to save relatives from disaster.

I went to a spiritualist church séance and messed around a bit with a Ouija board at home. The first left me unconvinced and the second scared me half to death. In retrospect I don't know how much of that was real and how much my sister and I conjured up but I felt I might be moving to the dark side and unleashing more than I could handle.

Interviewing John in India more than 40 years later for this book, I realise he had quickly moved towards a much more subtle and sophisticated exploration of spiritual reality and self-exploration. My focus had turned to a serious boyfriend and John and I moved in different circles for a while.

College left me with a slightly better understanding of English literature, an awakened sense of social justice from sociology, below-average typing speeds and very rudimentary shorthand skills.

The life questions continued beneath the surface but the way to find answers was still far from clear. I saw an emptiness and superficiality in the lives that people were living and idealised a spiritual alternative I couldn't yet define.

Perhaps, like many people, I settled with Hamlet's sense that 'There are more things in heaven and earth, Horatio, than are dreamt of in your philosophy,' but I had no clear way of finding out what those things were or if they were accessible to me as a real experience that would also stand the scrutiny of critical analysis.

2

INDIA BECKONS

I WASN'T A WISE TEENAGER. In fact, I was like a ship on a stormy sea, with intense emotions that heaved and threw me around on gigantic waves and left me in the doldrums when everything seemed grey and pointless on damp English days.

The poems I wrote at this time were deeply critical of the world in which I was living and I saw myself as prostituting my writing skills in my new job as an advertising copywriter. Even though I was enjoying the creative crowd I worked with and relished having escaped from school to the adult world at a vibrant time when anything seemed possible, I couldn't find meaning in what I was doing.

I married at 18 to someone I loved and we had many special times but not the level of real communication that can take a relationship from romance to deeper understanding.

It always seemed something was missing in me. It wasn't filled by marriage, job, having a house, friends, going to the pub, parties or any of the normal activities. Only drinking or sex temporarily removed the problem by blurring the harsh edges of reality, and I enjoyed quite a bit of both.

One Sunday late in 1975, I was walking in the forestry commission land behind our terraced house in Sussex when an idea struck me. I said to my husband, Jake, "Let's go to India". I knew very little about India at the time, except from childhood books of snake charmers, rickshaws and elephants. Perhaps I was influenced by news pictures of the Beatles with the Maharishi Mahesh Yogi in India or subconscious memories of Dad's tales of the 'men in the Himalayas' and sensed there might be something there I needed.

Next day, I started researching how we could drive to India and, despite having struggled to get our foot on the property ladder with our little house, the idea took off. We prepared to sell our home and drive into the unknown.

Six months later, we set off with a few supplies in a red Ford Transit van, which a friend had converted to provide a few cupboards and sleeping space in the back. Our only guidebook was the BIT guide—a cheaply-produced contemporary guide on cheap places to stay, pitfalls to avoid and details of people in local jails who had been busted for drugs at various Asian border crossings. We were probably naive and blindly courageous in equal measures.

The distances were vast and there was a genuine feeling of exploring new territory and being totally alone in unfamiliar (and occasionally threatening) places. Without the mobile phones and internet that keep travellers connected today, we were adrift a very long way from home.

When we met up with others on the so-called hippy trail at camping spots in major centres, it was an opportunity to swap vital intelligence on the road ahead and on handling border crossings. We learnt that we needed to have *baksheesh* for the guards in Afghanistan to stop them pulling everything apart—they got our last bottle of wine, which we'd saved since France—but play it straight and definitely don't have any drugs crossing into Iran.

Sadly, my diaries of the travels seem to have been focused predominantly on what we ate and on health issues rather than being a comprehensive travelogue but they capture some of the joy at a whole new world opening up as we travelled through Europe, Turkey, Iran, Afghanistan and Pakistan. We often deviated from the most direct route, as we had the luxury of our own vehicle, and we picked up a few other travellers along the way.

India itself was initially a disappointment. The squalor and poverty hit us immediately, despite our gradual acclimatisation to different conditions as we had progressed through Asia. Women sat at the roadside picking nits from the hair of dirty children dressed in rags. For many miles there was nothing but roadside shacks, dust and dirt. Anywhere we stopped, we were quickly surrounded by flies and crowds of staring faces, which I found disconcerting and uncomfortable.

Places to eat served very meagre rations of dahl and chai while we sat on *charpoys* beside the road. When we tried to supplement the diet with any fresh fruit and vegetables, we found they were pocked by the ravages of pests and humid climate. And the monsoon was breaking. Driving through blinding torrents of rain on unfamiliar roads amid a turbulent river of bicycles, pedestrians and ox carts was demanding to say the least.

But the biggest disappointment for me was that the wisdom I'd expected to find revealed in India was not obvious. If anything, the people we met seemed greedy to have a part of the materialistic life we'd escaped from. A poem I wrote to India at the time said, 'You'd swap your soul for a radio'.

During our travels, I read *The Master Game* by Robert De Ropp, which seemed to point to the dimension of life I wanted. He built on Maslow's hierarchy of needs to talk about the self-actualisation that was humanity's greatest potential—once the basic needs of food, shelter, sex and income were taken care of. Achieving this was the 'Master Game'.

I was keen to find guidance but really didn't know where in India to look. Our naivety and lack of research were obvious factors in the failure to connect with any ashram or teacher but nor did we find the fellow traveller or noticeboard that might have given us a pointer in the right direction. The Indian tradition says that when the disciple is ready, the guru appears. Perhaps I wasn't ready, despite being hungry.

Considering our lack of research and the absence of comprehensive guide books, it's amazing how much we did see. We stumbled upon the Golden Temple in Amritsar quite by accident when we were driving through the town and saw a signpost in English.

We tramped around Delhi in mind-melting heat and headed off to the Taj Mahal. We parked for the evening in Agra, somewhere close to the famous monument. Even after seeing dozens of pictures, I was unprepared for its magical presence, visible in the early morning light. Its glowing marble was such a contrast to the drabness and poverty of the surrounding town.

We somehow found our way to Varanasi (then called Benares) despite having no previous idea of its significance. There, I glimpsed an amazing other-world that partly intrigued me and partly scared me. A guide led us down endless, narrow alleyways between high, overhanging buildings. Every alley was lined with the simplest hole-in-the-wall shops, which sold coloured powders, garlands and brass icons. Many Indians hurried past and I could sense the growing excitement in pilgrims reaching their destination.

Eventually we emerged at the River Ganges, which was lapping high on the *ghats* after monsoon rains. Bodies on wooden stretchers covered in bright orange cloth were being carried past us for burning. Strange-smelling smoke made the cloying heat and humidity even more intense. It was fascinating and repelling in equal measure.

We took a boat-tour on the brown swirling water in the late afternoon. Another dead body floated by, face-down, bloated and somehow inhuman in its lifelessness.

I sensed the thousands of years of life and death here in one of the oldest cities on earth. But it offered me no windows to the spirituality beyond the surface of what I was seeing.

These days, it's hard to imagine arriving somewhere without having explored it from every angle on the internet first. Then, it was like Alice going down the rabbit-hole and emerging somewhere quite unexpected with no clue of how to make sense of it all. Although I was looking for deeper understanding, I was little more than a tourist passing through.

In the week that followed, we drove up steep, picturesque roads in Nepal, where waterfalls plunged hundreds of feet down the steep slopes beside us. Precarious rope footbridges swung across deep ravines of rushing water. People carrying loads stabilised by straps around their foreheads watched and waved as our red van went past.

In Kathmandu, I relished the medieval atmosphere and being in a meeting-place of travellers from around the world who gathered in little restaurants and the famous pie shop.

After a week or two, I got very sick with dysentery. We were van-camping in the grounds of a guesthouse, which was not the ideal place to be sick. I was spending half the nights in a very basic outdoor toilet where mosquitoes and a large rat came to visit. In the day, I curled up on the floor of the van, feeling like death.

Eventually I checked in to a room in the guesthouse and I lay there for a few more days, not eating but occasionally drinking a sickly pineapple juice. I made constant trips between toilet and bed, driven by griping stomach pains.

We went to a local hospital for a stool test. They said I could stay but it reminded me of something from a book about Florence Nightingale I had as I child. Sick and bandaged people were lying on mattresses everywhere in a dirty-looking building. I thought I might not get out alive, so I went back to the guest house.

Jake started to get desperate as I wasn't improving. Eventually, he went to the British Embassy for recommendations.

The recommendation was a local herbalist who mixed up all sort of strange pills in a clinic, which Jake said was more like a witch-doctor's waiting room. The herbalist came to my hotel room and felt my pulse. By then, I hadn't eaten anything for more than a week. He asked if my ears were aching and I shook my head, thinking we might have a communication problem. He prescribed some huge, greenish pills with the consistency of compressed hay.

I thought nothing more of his comments about my ears until a week or so later when his pills had turned the tide and I was back on my feet again. We had walked up a hillside to a stupa with its eye looking out across the valleys below and prayer flags flying. By the time we reached the top, not only was I out of breath but my ears were also aching dreadfully. We returned to the herbalist for some more pills and they cleared the earache after a few more days.

Our money was running out. We had spent more on petrol than we'd anticipated and the months in Europe had been expensive. After selling our van in Kathmandu, we continued our journey back the way we'd come. The first leg back to Kabul was with an American woman with a mini-bus and then we travelled by local, long-distance buses.

We stopped in Kabul for a few days and took a trip to Bamiyan and Band-e-Amir, the region where the giant Buddhas in the cliffs towered over tiny villages, before the Taliban destroyed them in later years. It was a surreal landscape. At Band-e-Amir, incredibly bright blue lakes shimmered in the brilliant light of a dry, barren moonscape. I've never been anywhere else like it.

One morning, in a white-walled and sparse room in Kabul, I woke with no memory and no knowledge of who I was. I could see the room and was fully conscious but there was absolutely no mental activity to tell me anything or to make sense of my surroundings.

I was aware of my beingness and vaguely aware that it belonged to someone but who I was, or where I was, remained beyond reach. I was an instrument of open-eyed perception without name, past or future. This strange state lasted no more than a couple of minutes—not very long but a huge gap compared with the usual, almost-instantaneous upload of a sense of self and memories.

It was more than 30 years before 'Julia' started disappearing again.

On my return from India, I developed hepatitis A and spent 10 days in hospital with eyes of yellow and stools of clay.

We rented a little cottage with fields behind it and Jake went to work as a taxi driver as a fill-in. Our huge adventure faded into memory and I shivered through winter, baking bread and convalescing after my illness.

I hadn't given up on the spiritual search and followed various trails opened up by reading—including trying to meditate on my own. My friend John had also recently returned from India, where he'd visited the Rajneesh ashram in Poona (now Pune). He looked glowing and I felt quite envious of whatever he'd found there.

He lent me a book with some meditation techniques and I settled on a humming meditation—a phase of humming, before a stage of silence. I don't think I really understood quite what I was trying to achieve by meditation and was looking for earth-shattering experiences and out-of-this-world revelations. Sometimes the sunlight did seem brighter, the garden more vividly real and the mind pleasantly subdued when I'd finished. But it wasn't the Road to Damascus experience I'd been going for.

Six months after our return, my marriage broke up and I started a new phase living and working in London. I find it hard to remember now exactly why we split up, other than having grown somewhat apart in our interests. The trip to India had awakened a passion for adventure in me but I think he had had enough and wanted to settle back into an ordinary life.

When he dropped me off at my new bedsit in St John's Wood in London, part of me was in a total panic. I reassured myself that if I could survive without him for a minute, I could survive without him for ten minutes; if I could survive without him for ten minutes, I could survive without him for an hour. And there are only 16 waking hours in a day. All I had to do was live minute by minute and I would be okay. It was an important lesson, born of emotional necessity.

At first it was a trial separation with weekend visits to see each other but, after a few months, he met someone else. "She needs me, Julia," he said. "You don't need me". And all that time I had been trying to be an independent woman and to keep my clingy tendencies under control! Initially, I was devastated but, deep down, I knew there wasn't a way forward for us.

A new relationship with Ellis, a man who I was working with and who would become a major part of my life, helped make a lonely time in London easier. Before long, we were in love. It was a time of passionately discovering each other, even though circumstances were not always easy. He was married but not happy and our relationship had to be secret from everyone. When love consumes us, nothing else seems to matter. Every moment together was precious—an experience of living in the present that was available without effort.

About nine months after we met, he left his wife.

Our initial move to live together was a mattress on a friend's floor in Ladbroke Grove. This was followed by a tiny, very basic, one-bedroom flat in Bromley. In this first-floor space overlooking a busy road, the dining table was a card table, the fridge dated back decades and the cupboard-sized, ancient bathroom was painted a claustrophobic shade of murky blue.

It was a romantic time. Being together was more important than where we were living. And we were together day and night, commuting to work together, putting the travel industry to rights in the day and happy in each other's arms at night. Ellis's two young boys visited every other weekend and suddenly I had to adjust to the reality of being a part-time stepmother to boisterous, and often hostile, children. That part wasn't easy.

At one stage, Ellis returned to his wife to live for a week or two because she wasn't coping and was bombarding him with late-night phone calls. I toughed it out but I think I was quite shaken. At one point during that period, I suffered something close to a breakdown.

I pulled out of a travel agents' trip to Mauritius at the last minute because I was convinced that I was going to die if I went. I also remember sobbing uncontrollably in the car one day for no very good reason when we'd gone for a drive to the coast.

Struggling somewhat with everyday life challenges may have added to my need to find a meaning or purpose in it all. I looked for new possibilities around the London area.

I visited the Gurdjieff centre in Buckinghamshire, taking a train to the end of the Metropolitan Line. Gurdjieff was an Armenian mystic who lived from 1866-1949 and established a famous school of esoteric work in Paris in the 1920s. The Gurdjieff centre I visited emphasised 'self-remembrance' and advised various exercises for waking from the hypnotic, automated state we usually operate in. These included avoiding saying certain words they'd randomly chosen each week. I might walk around remembering not to say 'awful, hope, milk, very, sweet, animal' one week and 'nice, bright, baby, run, probably and sad' another week.

Again, the results were very subtle for someone looking for a transformative and transcendental signpost.

I did a weekend meditation retreat somewhere out in Oxfordshire, where sitting meditation alternated with ultra-slow Zen walking and communing with trees. The whole thing was excruciatingly boring and I wished I'd stayed at home with Ellis and gone to the pub!

I also visited the Rajneesh meditation centre in Chalk Farm in London, because I could definitely see something different in John's eyes since he'd become a Rajneesh *sannyasin*—traditionally someone who has renounced the world to dedicate himself, or herself, to a spiritual life.

I arrived in my city corporate clothes and climbed the stairs to a warehouse space where there were many people in orange robes and wearing a *mala*—holy beads (in this case 108 wooden beads with a picture of Rajneesh). The guy leading the meditation also had that depth and shine in his eyes that I'd seen in John's. I wanted some of what they had!

The meditation was a shock. This was not all about sitting quietly—or at least not until the end. The Dynamic Meditation has a number of strange stages including jumping in the air and shouting 'hoo' for 10 minutes, followed by 10 minutes of catharsis where everyone wailed and screamed and growled like wild animals. The air stunk of sweat and I stayed at the edge, wary of all these tortured beings expressing their anger, anguish and animosity. I feebly stomped around and made a few primitive sounds but I couldn't seem to contact the raw emotion that was consuming everyone else. Surely this wasn't the path to that angelic smile and those shining eyes?

Despite this unnerving experience, this was the best lead I had. Although I avoided going back for another meditation, I read the Rajneesh books that John lent me and found much inspiration. They also introduced me to the concept of 'enlightenment'—a very desirable state of bliss and ultimate knowledge. This wasn't a nebulous heaven in an afterlife but heaven on earth. It was supposedly achievable through practicing meditation until the breakthrough moment when all delusion drops away.

I particularly remember one Zen story about the nun Chiyono, who studied for many years but was unable to attain enlightenment. One moonlit night, she was carrying an old pail filled with water. As she watched the full moon's reflection in the water, suddenly the bamboo strips that held the pail together broke. The water gushed away and Chiyono was enlightened. She wrote a poem:

In this way and that I tried to save the old pail
Since the bamboo strip was weakening and about to break
Until at last the bottom fell out.
No more water in the pail!
No more moon in the water!

It was mysterious but enticing and offered a very different perspective from my Christian upbringing.

I carried on doing the occasional quiet meditations at home from time to time—eventually in our own terraced house in Tonbridge—but it was a minor part of my life. Work and regular social drinking consumed the next few years.

They were very happy times with long walks over the Downs; full-moon, summer nights deep in the Kent countryside; and snowy winters with walks in crisp snow. Ellis made me feel safe and loved. His emotional depth spoke to mine and we worked well together in many ways. I sometimes imagined us sitting on a park bench together in old age, still in love and caring for each other. Looking back, I realised those years were some of the times of greatest security and simple loving relationship in my life. But I was still too young to fully appreciate that domestic bliss doesn't always come that easily.

We had some amazing trips together too, from walking in the Pennines to explorations in Kenya. Foreign trips were made easier thanks to our travel agency discounts.

The yearning for a deeper truth hadn't gone away but, if the way to get there was through years of that exhausting and hellish meditation, I wasn't ready for it yet. Although I didn't see a path forward in that search, I questioned most of the conventional things I did. I bought a cine camera but felt I should be managing without material possessions. I went to overseas travel conferences but felt I was an outsider amongst people talking about their superficial lives. I had a wonderful trip to Australia on a travel agents' educational, where I totally identified with a man who we visited on Dunk Island. He had been a Sydney stockbroker but was now living in a hut and eating oysters off the rocks.

As time passed, I wanted to have children but Ellis was against starting another family. I began to wonder if there was a future for us. I'd always seen children as part of my life at some point.

Apart from love, nothing seemed very real and even that was less tangible once it fell into everyday routine and mundane living. On one particularly bleak winter commute home, I dreamt of staying on the train to Dover, catching a cross-channel ferry and travelling away to exotic places without telling anyone where I'd gone.

Instead, I eventually booked a three-week holiday in India to check out the Rajneesh ashram for myself.

3

CULT OR SPIRITUAL COMMUNE?

JOHN, WHO WAS BACK IN INDIA, met me in the ashram van at Bombay. As the ashram driver, he was visiting printers in the city with a female *sannyasin* called Yatri.

Although India hadn't been my favourite place on my original travels and although I was tired from not having slept much on the overnight flight, I was suddenly excited to be back there. The warm air and smells of spices and open drains hit me with a blast of forgotten familiarity but also promised new possibilities.

After touring printers' workshops in old buildings with an almost Dickensian feel, where John was picking up ashram books, we had tea at the majestic Taj Hotel and set off for Poona in the early evening.

I dozed and, somewhere along the way, John stopped the van on a ridge as we ascended the Western Ghats. We got out to look at the sky. I had never seen stars so magnificent. Here, there was a sense that the sky was a deep and infinite dome, rather than the ceiling it appeared in England. It was as if someone had, literally, taken the lid off my world.

Sometime late that night, I settled onto a mattress at Yatri's place in Poona and slept. I woke to a room reminiscent of the 1930s. The bathroom was of a similar era with an ancient bath, a vintage basin and a toilet with a chain-pull cistern fixed high on the wall.

There was also a magic wardrobe. Perhaps I was sleep-deprived but it appeared to me like something from a fantastic childhood tale. It has always stuck in my memory with exceptional clarity. When she opened the doors, it was full of her flowing *sannyasin* clothes in every shade of orange, apricot, red, maroon, saffron and cerise. I felt as if I had stepped into another world and that, by putting on clothes such as these, I might be transformed—rather as magic cloaks in fairy tales make the wearer invisible.

Visiting the ashram next morning was both amazing and a little stressful. Was I following the right etiquette? Was I holy enough? What might happen to me here? Within the pretty tropical gardens in a leafy area of old Poona, it was a lovely oasis of calm but not of solemnity. People seemed to be smiling and chatting, and John (who was now known as Devadas) showed me around.

Sadly, the guru was to evade me a bit longer. There was a chicken-pox outbreak and Bhagwan Shree Rajneesh was not giving his usual morning lectures. This was something of a disappointment. I felt I needed to see the man himself to know if this was really an avenue for me. Now I would not have the opportunity to look into his eyes and see if they touched me with honesty or love.

But I was here and there was no point in wasting the time. I discovered the Kundalini Meditation—done in the late afternoons and a gentler experience than the dreaded Dynamic Meditation—and I also enrolled for something called an 'Enlightenment Intensive' group, which was due to start a few days later. Four days to reach an experience of enlightenment sounded like a very good deal to me!

I joined the group full of anticipation. Each day of the timetable started at about 5am with Dynamic Meditation with about 100 other group participants. I struggled with the physical demands of it and with the bedlam that broke out in the cathartic stage. It was almost enough to make me resign on the first morning but then we settled into the format of the days.

We sat on the floor and each person sat opposite a partner for 10 minutes and answered the question 'Who am I?'. The other person wasn't allowed to respond or speak, only to make eye contact. Then, they had a turn to answer the question for 10 minutes before everyone moved on to a new partner and repeated the process. This questioning continued until late in the evening, broken only by a slow walking-meditation after lunch and meal breaks for very light sustenance and herbal teas.

To start with, most people's tone was chatty, telling the other person about their lives. Then, after a few rounds, we slowly began to reveal some of our deeper challenges and difficulties. Some sessions became more analytical, maybe speculating on what was constant or even eternal in us. Eventually, the process became annoyingly repetitive and most people seemed to be struggling.

I didn't understand what the idea was and how this was going to get me enlightened. I also had a caffeine-withdrawal headache and was hot and hungry! The first day was followed by a night sleeping on the flat roof of the ashram building with dozens of other people. We were woken before dawn for Dynamic Meditation and breakfast of an apple, an orange and lemongrass tea. Then, the 'Who am I?' question began again.

I survived two days and nights but couldn't face Dynamic Meditation on the third day. This was no way to spend my precious holiday. I resigned, despite efforts from the group leader to persuade me to stay. I went and sat in the ashram garden in the early morning and the bliss of life washed over me. Bright flowers, exotic birds, the caress of warm air—everything was so vivid and fresh, as if it had been just created. My thoughts seemed to be moving in slow motion. I sat still and drank in the loveliness of life.

That evening, John and his Mexican girlfriend, Maria, came to check on me at my lodgings to make sure I was okay.

Later, I understood the purpose of the group was to get beyond mental activity and self-concepts to a direct experience but, at the time, I felt frustrated that nothing was becoming any clearer. Either this ashram was a false trail or I was failing in the opportunity to achieve a transcendental breakthrough.

Even in the limited time I was there, the regular meditation, listening to taped lectures in 'Buddha Hall' and getting to know some of the people there was a positive experience. By the time I left, I felt I understood a little better what it was all about. But I couldn't know for sure until I'd seen the guru himself.

Another year passed back in England. I tried to settle back into daily life but the ashram experience hadn't left me. I knew I needed to go and spend longer and see this Bhagwan for myself. In early 1981, I gave up my job, said goodbye to Ellis—with many tears and much trepidation—and set off for six months in the ashram. Ellis gave me a book for my journey—*The Serpent of Paradise, The story of an Indian pilgrimage* by Miguel Serrano. It was the most precious possession in my red rucksack as I headed off into the unknown.

The next few months were an amazing and unforgettable time but it wasn't always easy. I felt the awful pain of separation from Ellis and fear of the unknown as I settled into a makeshift one-room home with rush-mat walls under a brick building. Loud radios kept me awake late into the evening. But, however difficult, I knew I had to make the most of this opportunity.

I soon got into the habit of rising before dawn, taking an auto-rickshaw to the ashram and joining people—mostly westerners in various shades of red and orange—streaming from every direction towards Buddha Hall for the morning lecture. Musicians played for a while before Bhagwan himself appeared—a gentle-looking man in his late 40s with greying beard and dressed in a simple white robe. He walked onto the stage with hands together in *namaste* and a beaming smile that conveyed both joy and contentment.

By the time I arrived, Rajneesh was already establishing a reputation as an unconventional guru and a great orator.

Respected journalist, Bernard Levin of *The Times,* had visited the previous year and written a series of articles that acknowledged Bhagwan as both a compelling unscripted speaker and a living source of spiritual knowledge. Levin was also impressed by the ashram, *sannyasins* and the alternative vision on offer. Sadly, Levin was the subject of many jokes as the result of this and it was even mentioned in his obituaries in 2004. *The Guardian* said, "This embracing of odd ideas led him on to writing articles in praise of the spurious guru Bhagwan Rajneesh"[1].

Today Rajneesh, who died in 1990, is known as Osho—after he changed his name sometime in the 1980s. He still creates strongly divided opinions. Conventional wisdom dismisses him as a crazy, cult guru and some ex-*sannyasins* wrote controversial exposés of the awful events that later engulfed the movement in Oregon USA. Despite this, his books are offered in profusion at Indian airports and in many bookshops around the world. The ashram in Poona was reinvented after his death and still attracts tens of thousands of visitors a year, some of whom are *sannyasins* from the early days. In 2018, the *Wild, Wild Country* documentary about the Oregon phase was one of the year's biggest Netflix hits.

When I was at the ashram in 1981, the infrastructure around Rajneesh was relatively simple and, although he was deeply loved and almost hero-worshipped by *sannyasins*, this was no different from the reverence Indians traditionally show their gurus and holy men—or the way Catholics turn out for a drive-by of the pope-mobile.

Thousands of people were coming every week and, while there was the peer pressure of enthusiasm, there was nothing that I would call 'brainwashing' and no organised effort to coerce people into staying. If anything, the model was to stay a while and then go, as there was great competition for a permanent place as an ashram worker.

To me, it felt as I imagined it would have been around Jesus when he started to preach and when he encouraged disciples to leave their old lives behind, "But Jesus said to him, Follow me; and let the dead bury their dead" [2].

While I can't remember any blinding flash of certainty on the first morning that I saw Rajneesh, I was quickly seduced by his humour, insights and answers to disciples' questions. For the first time in my life, someone was answering the deepest questions I had in a way that made absolute sense. Within the 90-minute talk, I might find myself laughing one moment and crying with relief and gratitude the next, or sitting in a state of stillness and total acceptance. His ability to speak authoritatively on many spiritual traditions confirmed my long-held intuition that all religions shared roots in some basic truth that had become reinterpreted in different ways.

Meanwhile, during the days, I participated in various therapy and meditation groups or spent time with other people I'd met. I had a pass to go to the ashram workers' quarters to meet Devadas, and later an Argentine man with whom I developed a close relationship. I moved from the rather ramshackle accommodation to a unit in town where I shared a kitchen and bathroom with other *sannyasins*. In the evenings I went for milkshakes with a 10-year-old *sannyasin* girl, Marianne, whose father also lived in the apartment.

My wardrobe morphed from the turquoise dungarees of my first visit to shades of red and pink. In my red jump-suit, I rode pillion with my Argentine friend on his motorbike. We took trips out from Poona, including a long weekend at Mahabeleshawar hill station. At Mahabeleshawar, I had a distinct feeling I knew the place. Perhaps it was the enduring reminders of the British Raj in the décor and menus with Anglo-Indian fare but, as I wandered around the colonial graveyard, I had a strange feeling that I was buried there.

Another day we rode out to a lake amongst the hills for a swim. It was a time of adventure and elation as well as spiritual focus.

Music was a big part of life around the ashram too—both meditation music and the sound of people playing guitars and singing the popular songs of the time—Neil Young, Cat Stevens or John Lennon. In *sannyasin*-run restaurants around town, western music played and lights twinkled in the trees as we ate excellent food and swapped stories with people from around the world.

I felt at home. These were my people. I walked with a new lightness and pleasure in being alive.

One of the aspects that made Rajneesh so controversial, especially amongst Indians, was his attitude to sex. This has often been very superficially understood because, essentially, he was simply saying that sex shouldn't be suppressed, as it is by most religions. He said that the best way to transcend its hold and transform it is to experience it and go through it.

"The work of a *sannyasin* consists of transforming sexual energy into prayer. That day is the greatest in your life when sex is transformed into prayer, when your sex has no sexuality in it but becomes prayerful. My *sannyas* is not a renunciation of life but a transformation."[3] Similarly, he said, "Go on moving higher and higher—don't get entangled with the lower. I am not condemning the lower, remember. I am simply saying that the goal will not be fulfilled. Enjoy food but remember God. Enjoy relationship but remember God. Enjoy sex but remember *samadhi*."[4]

Inevitably this led to him being dubbed 'the Sex Guru' by sex-obsessed tabloid media, and film crews arrived in Poona wanting to film the *Tantra* Group, which was only one of scores of different therapy and self-exploration groups on offer. It wasn't even open to people until they had completed a certain number of other groups—no doubt to discourage opportunistic visitors.

Of course, there was plenty of sex going on around the place too. Many attractive people, who had grown up in the 1960s and 1970s, coming together with ideals of love and non-possessiveness, rather than fidelity, were more than open to exploring what was on offer. That was no different than it would have been on an under-35s holiday in Ibiza! Inevitably, there were also some Rajneesh followers who enjoyed shocking the establishment and were very happy to emphasise the controversial and the sexual.

I had always trusted the objectivity of the BBC television

station in England until, not long after my return from Poona, I saw a program they had made on the 'Sex Guru'. So much was exaggerated and out-of-context, creating a picture of non-stop orgies encouraged by a sex-obsessed guru. This was not the Poona I had visited. It totally discredited anything I said to my parents, friends and work colleagues about the spiritual nature of my visit to India. It also made it very hard to show public allegiance to Rajneesh without ridicule, animosity or knowing winks. I had a small taste of what religious persecution would feel like.

But the worst controversy was still in the future and, for the first time, I was starting to experience life from an 'enhanced' state of consciousness. This wasn't a psychedelic world or a world of visions, which I'd once imagined as the confirmation I'd been looking for. It was a world where thoughts and time sometimes stood still to make the ordinary world so much more vivid and pregnant with a feeling of rightness and intrinsic value.

Often, walking beneath the banyan trees full of parrots flying home at dusk, after I'd done a Kundalini Meditation, there were no more questions but only a deep sense of delight and peace. I was at home in a way I had never been in my life before.

Once, after a mango and curd breakfast with my Argentine friend, I felt almost as if I were walking a few feet above the ground and I was part of a transcendent perfection. All thoughts were in distant slow-motion for hours afterwards.

Another time, I was in the market in the afternoon buying bananas and I suddenly felt a deep loving connectedness with everyone there. It was an intense feeling and knowledge that we are all one, and that the ground of this oneness is Love.

Such proclamations may sound like clichéd hippie aphorisms but the knowledge was unquestionable, incomparable and beyond anything I had ever imagined.

4

COMMITMENT, CONFUSION, COMMITMENT...

A FEW MONTHS PASSED and I was still uncertain about taking the leap to be a *sannyasin*. To me, it was a very big decision but friends there said I was taking it all too seriously; that it was playful or a love affair. I was resistant to becoming part of the 'club' in strangely coloured clothes and wearing a mala. My spirituality felt like an inner perspective not something I needed to proclaim by marking myself out and separating myself from ordinary people.

Eventually, I was convinced that perhaps I was missing the deeper experience by my lack of surrender. I put my application form in at the office—a surprisingly bureaucratic requirement for a spiritual life-decision!

On 15 April, I took *sannyas* in a ceremony at the evening *darshan*. I took the option of including my original name rather than a total name change so became Ma Dhyan Julia. For me, it was a commitment to my spiritual life ahead of anything else and an acknowledgement of Rajneesh as my spiritual master. "*Sannyas* is a commitment—a commitment to know yourself, a commitment to risk all for this exploration."[5]

This didn't mean that he was personally directing my actions—only the closest disciples had direct contact by this time—or that I would have done anything against my own values at his request. My knowledge of him and trust in his teaching made me certain he would never have requested anything that endangered my life or that of others.

> *A Master is one who will not tell you to follow him, but he will certainly tell you to be silently with him. It has nothing to do with following. A real, authentic master does not want to create pseudo replicas, carbon copies; he helps you to discover your original face. He will not impose any structure on you; on the contrary, he will help you to get rid of imposed structures.*[6]

He specifically told us not to follow him—or anyone. "Listen but don't follow. Listen but follow your insight; don't follow others' advice. Listen certainly, very meditatively. Try to understand what they are trying to convey to you—but if you start following blindly you will never attain to your own intelligence."[7]

I remember him speaking of the Jonestown massacre and explaining why it could never happen in his community. Perhaps if he had continued his dynamic dialogue with disciples, the commune would not have unravelled amidst crime, scandal and legal proceedings five years later but, in

May 1981, he went into silence, only communicating his wishes through a few appointed women.

The charismatic lectures were replaced by *satsangs* in silence. At first, I experienced a feeling of loss that he had stopped speaking so soon after I had found him. Then, I found the silent *satsangs* created a beautiful environment to meditate and be present, while the tropical birds called from the trees and the train coming into Poona station whistled in the distance.

Not long after this, it was announced that the ashram was moving to a new location that would make it possible for many more of the tens of thousands of *sannyasins* to spend extended time. We understood there were also various background Indian political problems going on and that the move also had something to do with that.

For me, it was an opportunity to experience working as an ashram worker by joining the expanded army of volunteers that was packing up huge stores of books and making other preparations for the next phase.

At times in my childhood, I had thought of being a nun. Probably many girls in convent schools do. There was something about the nuns' devotion that appealed but I didn't like the idea of rejecting the world and being shut away with other women who spoke in whispers and spent long periods on their knees. Even before I fully understood the implications of chastity, I felt it was better to be in the ordinary world of both sexes.

As part of the Rajneesh *sannyasin* community, I had the devotional commitment and shared community of a religious order but also the openness to all of life that I instinctively felt was a healthy orientation.

I also loved the diversity of people I met. Whether the red-robed person I talked to was a lawyer from Canada, a cleaner from Colombia, an architect from Milan or a welder from Manchester, we all spoke a common language. Not only had I found a spiritual direction that resonated with my own experience but I was part of a brave new approach to society. It was an exhilarating mixture.

There were distressing times too. For ages I had been looking forward to a visit from Ellis and was keen to share my new perspectives with him. Then, the night before his visit, I realised I was also deeply attached to the Argentine man I had been spending a lot of time with. The greatest value I held at that time was 'be true to your feelings' but why were my feelings so confusing and creating such an impossible situation?

I sat up most of the night before Ellis arrived, agonising and talking to another *sannyasin* woman who was staying in the same apartment block.

One of the hardest and most painful things in life is knowing you are betraying someone's love but not being able to change what you are feeling. Having to confess the situation not long after Ellis stepped off the plane at Poona airport was excruciating. These days, a mobile phone call might have allowed some pre-warning but, at that time, even landline calls had to be booked well in advance at Poona GPO. Then, once booked, you turned up at the appointed time to wait for hours for an unpredictable connection.

The following few weeks were uncomfortable for us all. I tried to repair things with Ellis and we went away for a break to Matheran, another hill station, reached by a little train, but we both felt the shadow of another man in the background.

To his credit, Ellis made the best of this difficult time and explored some of the options Poona offered with an open mind. At the end of his holiday period, he returned to England and I continued my temporary life as an ashram worker.

Not too much later, my funds were running low and I very reluctantly faced the fact that I had to return to the UK. The journey to Bombay for my flight was with a heavy heart. In less than six months I had fallen in love with India as well as with this alternative way of life. The love affair with the Argentine man had run its course but we farewelled each other with loving affection. By coincidence, I flew out of India on the same flight that was carrying Rajneesh to the USA.

Whatever later emerged about Rajneesh and the *sannyasin* commune, I look back on those months in Poona as some of the most enjoyable and transformative in my life. I had had a real taste of something deeper and a glimpse of what lies beneath the busy everyday world.

I returned to Ellis and our shared house but inevitably things had changed.

For slightly less than a year, I tried to merge my old and new life with somewhat messy consequences.

Amazingly I managed to pick up freelance copywriting work despite turning up at clients' offices in strangely coloured suits and a mala. But some things were less easy to reinvent.

I tried to do Kundalini Meditation most afternoons but the music tape from Poona that defined the different stages reminded me how far away I was and often evoked yearning and nostalgia rather than peace.

Everything about England seemed small, enclosed, pale and petty in comparison with the colourful chaos of India, the wild hills, the heat and the world of potential I'd been living in.

I still loved Ellis but my old life felt flat and like being back in a box after having flown free for a while.

Maybe six months after my return, when visiting my sister in Brighton, I met another *sannyasin* on the street and discovered that there was a local commune starting there. I went one Sunday night to watch a video and who was there but my dear friend John, who was dating the centre leader! Our lives seemed to frequently intertwine.

After a few visits for video evenings and meditations, I asked to join the commune as a worker. This meant living in a shared house and donating all income to the commune and receiving £10 per week pocket money. It was a measure of my commitment to a spiritual life rather than any strong inclination to live communally.

Again, I left Ellis with regret, guilt, terror and anguished tears but a sense that I must do so to be true to myself. Sometimes I think 'separation' has been one of the big themes or lessons of my life. I've never managed to handle it cleanly without a backward glance and without trauma and regret at the possibilities lost.

During the months that followed, I was woken every morning by whoever was on morning-tea duty and I surrendered to the timetable and tasks allocated by the centre leaders. I continued my freelance work, because it was good income for the commune, but also took on cooking duties for the evening meal. There were three shared houses around the town and we all came together for dinner—about 15-20 people.

I really enjoyed creating interesting, wholesome food to serve my fellow *sannyasins.* I have enduring memories of chopping mounds of vegetables with different helpers each day as Van Morrison played in the background.

I also made many lasting friends from the extended *sannyasin* community in the town when we came together for celebration days or meditations. I still have a photo of me and a beautiful woman friend, Atosh, standing behind the large cakes we'd baked for a celebration day. The words 'Love, Life, Laughter' were piped on the cakes in icing.

It was a creative, sociable and often crazy time. There were commune politics of course but generally the shared commitment and high standards of home-keeping made it a positive place to be. Moments of deep insight arose from time to time amid the everyday routines.

One particular evening, I was dancing at a party, after appearing in our reinvented version of *A Midsummer Night's Dream,* when I had a few moments of mind-shattering insight. I knew with absolute certainty that everything in my life had led to this moment and that this moment was absolute perfection—as is every other moment, if only we could see it.

Such insights may last only minutes but seem to be of a different quality, reality and intensity than everyday life experiences. This particular one was so intense and unquestionable that it remained a touchstone for a long time when life seemed to be very imperfect and pointlessly cruel.

I think it was during this period that I also went to hear Krishnamurti. He has been groomed by the Theosophists to be the 'New World Teacher' but had rejected the organisation and its esoteric doctrines. My first encounter was at his Brockwood Park School in Hampshire where he held talks in a large marquee on a sunny, summer weekend. Then, on another occasion, I went to hear him at a more formal venue in London. Krishnamurti attracted a more conventional crowd than Rajneesh—lots of older English ladies who might have been equally at home in the Women's Institute, it seemed to me at the time! He had a sweet and steady presence yet I couldn't quite grasp where he was coming from. His approach was more of a philosophical discussion and I felt that I was missing the point—which I probably was. In retrospect, I realise he was very good at unpicking preconceptions and taking a paring knife to imaginative spiritual ideas but I was looking for deep experiential moments and tangible guidance on getting them.

In 1982, I went to the Rajneesh First Annual World Celebration in Oregon, where the ashram had now been re-established. We had always celebrated a traditional Guru Purnima day around July—a traditional Indian festival at the full moon during monsoon when disciples go to honour their guru—but this was a totally new interpretation.

Amidst the wild, cattle-eroded hills of Oregon, an incredible amount of work had already been undertaken towards building a model city. In addition to a core 'mall' area, there were hundreds of A-frame timber homes for permanent residents, and thousands of temporary tents for festival visitors. A bus service with many old yellow school buses moved people around the extensive ranch. I was appalled and impressed in equal measure by the changes since Poona.

I was impressed by the vision that was carving very productive farms and businesses from a wild, over-grazed property and by the organisation that fed thousands of us on delicious home-grown organic meals in huge marquees. I was appalled by the commercialisation that was supporting it. The shops in the new mall not only featured a wonderful array of clothes in *sannyasin* colours and Rajneesh books but also a whole new range of Rajneesh memorabilia including key rings, hats, beer-holders, pens and even pillowcases with Rajneesh's picture on.

Bhagwan himself had had a makeover too. Gone was the simple white Indian robe, replaced by snazzy blue or black robes and a trade-mark, beanie-style hat.

There was also the afternoon 'drive-by' when Rajneesh drove a Rolls Royce along the dirt roads, which were lined with *sannyasin*s for kilometres. The fleet of Rolls Royces that he accumulated became a major point of criticism by the outside world and certainly raised questions for some disciples. While Rajneesh had always claimed poverty wasn't an essential part of spirituality, that riches weren't a problem only attachment to them was, and while the Rolls Royces were owned by the Foundation and not by him, the whole charade seemed ill-advised. Many enjoyed it as a game that Bhagwan was playing to shake up people's pre-conceived ideas and gain publicity for his message but my heart sank a little at what was developing.

Security was tighter too at the new mega-sized Buddha Hall, with select guards even carrying guns in the American way.

On Master's Day, Rajneesh appeared on the stage like a larger-than-life wizard, exactly as lightning flashed and thunder rolled around the dusty hills. Despite my misgivings, my relationship was to him and his teaching and I did my best to ignore the worrying precedents, to meditate and enjoy reuniting with old friends.

I took a ranch tour out through the vast vegetable fields, past the barns of hens, where a dreamy looking *sannyasin* girl sat with a hen on her lap stroking it blissfully. I volunteered to do some farm work but found the weeding hot and exhausting so I only did a day, reasoning that this was my only holiday for the year.

In the evenings, many people congregated at Zorba the Buddha restaurant or the disco, where we danced until late.

We were all proud of the amazing ecological transformation that our people had achieved on a piece of desolate land that farmers had rejected as being beyond redemption. It seemed symbolic of the possibility to transform ourselves, society and human interactions by working in harmony to achieve goals beyond individual selfish interests.

It was wonderful to meet up with old friends from Poona days too, including my Argentine lover who was now working there. There was still friendly warmth and affection between us as he took my hand to show me behind the scenes of some of the workers' areas.

I think it was the following year at the celebration that Ma Anand Sheela, the now notorious secretary to Bhagwan, gathered everyone for an orientation talk and said that various *sannyasins* (previously part of the inner circle) had been excommunicated and that we weren't to associate with them. Some people cheered. This rang loud alarm bells for me and I said to my travel companions that, if those excommunicated had been my friends, I would continue to associate with them.

I disliked Sheela and wondered if she was really speaking for Bhagwan or running things her own way.

By late in the English summer 1983, rules in the Brighton commune seemed to be getting petty too. We were told money was short at the central British commune in Suffolk, which took a cut of money we earned, and that there would be no more desserts with meals. We would also have to give up the different houses where people had separate rooms and move into dormitories in one of the bigger houses. Some of us were muttering about selling a few Rolls Royces so we could have our pudding!

On a personal level, I was also tiring of transient relationships and my biological clock was starting to ring alarm bells. I missed the stable love and closeness of being with Ellis. I yearned for the easy caring and tenderness we'd shared at our best. He was my best friend as well as a loving partner and who better to share the journey of parenthood?

He had also changed his mind about not wanting to have another child. We reunited with a sense of anticipation at the possibility of a baby and with renewed enthusiasm for our relationship. I didn't immediately leave the commune but went back to our original house at weekends and we had a mini 'honeymoon' in Venice.

This may sound crazy but, walking in Queen's Park in Brighton a few weeks later, I felt the presence of a new being around me and I knew I was pregnant before any physical signs suggested it.

Ellis and I decided to buy a house in Brighton where we could maintain contact with the *sannyasin* community but start a family home.

Life felt good and I still meditated regularly through my pregnancy, determined that my baby would have the best environment to grow in a calm and loving atmosphere. Ellis and I had a lovely holiday in Barbados, where I walked on the beach with a very pregnant belly. I felt at peace and full of happy anticipation.

I took off my mala when I went into labour in July 1984 and, once our daughter was born, I decided not to put it back on again. I felt that I couldn't have two masters and that this little person was going to be my first priority for the foreseeable future.

5

BEGINNINGS AND ENDINGS

AS ANY MOTHER KNOWS, having a baby changes everything. I was surprised how fiercely I guarded her and how carefully I controlled everything to ensure she had the best environment and never felt alone.

At first it was strange not to wear my *sannyasin* colours and I continued to have a wardrobe that was mostly reds, corals, pinks and peaches. I was still very close to many of the extended *sannyasin* community in Brighton and shared the same values. I liked it that so many friends dropped in and spent time with us, giving baby Lily a 'tribe' not only a nuclear family.

It was another close and blissful time with Ellis and it seemed as if life had finally settled into a contented and nurturing place where all the questions remained subdued.

As time progressed, news coming from the Rajneesh ranch in Oregon was increasingly weird. There were doubtless hostilities, discrimination and resistance from the authorities and local community from the very beginning but official messages from Sheela sounded almost paranoid. Where once our loving, joyful and spiritual community was going to set an example that melted local resistance, now it was necessary to have *sannyasin* candidates running for local government positions to ensure our vision prevailed and a team of lawyers to support the commune's needs.

Then, in a move that most people even within the organisation saw as a blatant attempt to stack the numbers in our favour in local elections, homeless people from cities around the US were picked up off the streets and offered homes in the commune.

Those who were living there then reported that some of the new residents found a fresh start and integrated but many were disruptive or criminal. Inevitably, the uncontrolled influx changed the ambience of the model city.

Then, we heard that Rajneesh had been taken into prison by the authorities on immigration charges. Although many of us had had doubts about the power plays within the organisation, there was still a feeling that Rajneesh himself was detached from all that. His arrest seemed an indignity and proof that nothing much changes in people's prejudice and that Jesus would be crucified again if he were here now.

After eventually putting in a technical plea of guilty to immigration charges, Rajneesh was released and expelled from the US. He stayed for a while at a disciple's home in Crete and, along with many other *sannyasins,* I made the journey (now with 18-month-old Lily in tow) to see him. I missed him by a couple of days but happily stayed for a holiday with friends from around the world.

After many other countries rejected Rajneesh, he returned to Poona.

Later, when the stories of what Sheela and her co-conspirators had done—including putting salmonella poisoning in local restaurant food and trying to poison Rajneesh's doctor—many *sannyasin*s felt betrayed and angry. Her actions had been the antithesis of the gentle new world we had envisaged.

Inevitably, it also raised questions about Rajneesh too. How much did he know? And even if he didn't know, shouldn't he have taken more responsibility for his disciples? It brought into question the whole concept of enlightenment too. For those of us who saw it as bestowing something akin to infallibility, we had to question how he was such a bad judge of character and so blind to what Sheela had been doing?

With plenty of books and the *Wild, Wild Country* documentary available, I don't want to get into an extended analysis of the phenomenon here but, for many of us, it was the end of an era. Others go to the reinvented Poona ashram two decades after his death.

Despite the dissolution of the dream society and the doubts cast on Rajneesh, I am far from alone in feeling gratitude for the insights and direction he gave me. On balance, I feel he had experienced the reality spoken of by mystics of many traditions but whether he lived in an unbroken state of enlightenment, I am now less sure. At the very least, he was an exceptionally-gifted, very poetic, master of philosophy with an amazing presence and deep psychological insight. He had the charisma and talent to present spiritual knowledge in a way that brought it to life and made it relevant for contemporary westerners.

I can still read his books and find insights and truth that have stood the test of time and of my own experience.

While I was searching for enlightenment and the knowledge I craved, life was teaching me its own lessons of impermanence, of the cycles of love and loss, of the futility of hoping for joy to last or pain to stay out of the picture.

The late 1980s were a time of painful transition for me, punctuated by an unexpected love affair that carried me on wings of bliss for a short while.

Not only was the Rajneesh period ending but my relationship with Ellis had also lost its way.

It wasn't that we were fighting but we seemed to be going through the motions and inhabiting separate worlds. He was away a lot—an important international business executive—and I was at home with a young child, rooted in an alternative culture that seemed far removed from his jet-setting circles.

There was still love there but it wasn't tangible to me most of the time. I felt as if I was stuck in a suburban rut that would move predictably to old age. I loved my daughter and enjoyed being a mother but how was I going to have adventures now?

I remember a day sitting in a pub outside Brighton when Ellis had had an operation on his foot, finding we didn't have much to say to each other and feeling as if the best days of my life had gone—that it would now be all about being a 'wife' at business functions and shopping at Waitrose every Saturday. I felt that all I had to look forward to was long, dark English winters and grey routine.

I think we papered over the cracks, hoped for the best and missed the opportunity to reinvent our relationship for the next phase. The Zeitgeist was against us too. I was moving in circles where one was more likely to follow a new opportunity rather than sit in a counsellor's office trying to understand each other's deeper needs and motivations. I was open to another man's arms—at first as a spontaneous diversion but a wiser person might have known that the ideal of open and 'non-possessive' relationship rarely ends happily.

There was a possibility for us to move as a family to Miami, where Ellis had been offered a job. I was very tempted. We looked at houses there together. I made lists of pros and cons for moving or staying. I counted the numbers of entries each side of the list, I weighted the entries according to their importance, agonised over the weights I gave each—and still I wasn't sure.

The warm weather and loyalty to Ellis called me but I didn't know how to rekindle our passion, or how to live without it. And the only lifeline to the part of me that seemed most real was the *sannyasin* community in Brighton. I think I probably avoided saying some of these things out loud for fear of hurting him but in that avoidance were the seeds of even greater hurt.

Perhaps with real honesty and better communication, we would have contacted what I was missing. That is something I'll never know because, while he was away and I continued to agonise over what to do for the best, a new man came into my life.

Love comes in different ways. I was strongly attracted to Chandragiri from the start. He moved on the periphery of the Brighton *sannyasin* community, visiting for functions from his home about an hour's drive away.

I chatted to him at the *sannyasin* disco one evening and, before long, he was a regular visitor. He fitted in easily, stimulated me with his intelligent conversation, made me laugh with his dry sense of humour and was great at sharing household chores and amusing Lily.

Inevitably, or at least inevitably at that time and place, we ended up as lovers.

This was quickly more than a casual flirtation and he was good at romance. He gave me a puzzle ring that symbolised all the pieces falling into place. He said that, when he'd caught my eye across the room at a party, he knew he wanted to spend the rest of his life with me.

A sense of absolute rightness seemed to settle over everything. There were no deeper questions, there was only merging into love. For all the effort at spiritual practice, there are few places one sees the divine as clearly as in the eyes of love.

I was probably a 'love junkie' in some ways, looking for an unsustainable level of 'aliveness' but I also knew that, at its best, love was another doorway to the transcendent.

For the second time, I faced Ellis coming back after a period apart to find I had turned to someone else. Those times of disappointing him were some of the worst and most excruciating moments in my life because he was so much a part of me. I could feel his pain like my own.

Looking back with more objectivity years later, it seems as if the two men in my life at that time had different parts of my heart, that they perhaps represented my own divided self—Ellis had the part that longed for home and constancy, for easy intimacy and lasting affection. Chandragiri represented the excitement and passion I seemed to need to feel alive.

Ellis arrived before Christmas and I put my love affair on one side to try to keep some semblance of a family Christmas for him and Lily. I rationalised that Chandragiri and I would have other Christmases and it was the least I could do.

As things worked out, the only other Christmas I had with Chandragiri was on the other side of the world years later and by then we were no longer lovers.

The next six months were full of daring dreams, only tempered by sadness that Ellis was hurting. I wished I could be what he wanted me to be in his life but I couldn't find the path back.

That April, while Lily stayed with Ellis in Miami for a few weeks, Chandragiri and I had a holiday in Mexico, where everything seemed magical and almost surreal. We climbed pyramids in an overgrown jungle, we drank tequilas in a beach bar on Isla Mujeres and we drove through the night in a hired VW Beetle, where a blizzard of moths slowed our progress for mile after mile.

With hubris I felt that I was finally on track and life was going to be an ongoing adventure. We planned to buy or manage a beach resort in Tuluum in Mexico, where living was cheap and where Lily could grow up speaking Spanish and be no further away from Ellis in Miami than she would be in England. (Tuluum was a tiny village with a couple of beach-hut developments and it's hard to believe it has become so huge and fashionable since then.)

Apart from being aware that Ellis was suffering really badly from our break-up and feeling his pain, I was happy. Happy with Chandragiri. Happy with my gorgeous daughter, who was a fun and intelligent little person. Happy that we were going to create a life together away from the rat-race in a sunny and special place. I was grateful for every day and, again with hubris, believed perhaps this was my reward for being true to myself, for not compromising for an easy life and for making all the difficult leaps of faith to follow my heart.

The fast unravelling of the seemingly idyllic relationship with Chandragiri was partly circumstances and partly no doubt the flaws in both of us that were bound to come to light eventually. Some would say it was my karma. The contributing factors are too personal and complex to analyse in detail here but, before the end of the year, it was my turn to have a broken heart as Chandragiri withdrew into a depressed state.

A big contributor was the fact he had lost most of his money and the cottages he had been investing in—the money had been his inheritance and it would have helped fund our new life plans. I didn't care about the money but he said he no longer felt the same about me. Maybe it was the depression talking and I should have stuck by him but it seemed he was pushing me away and that I had no choice but to be pushed.

In my heart, I didn't give up for a long time and there was a huge hole where the love and dreams had been. Even before the final decision, as I felt him begin to become more distant, I collapsed with pneumonia and was in bed for two or three weeks. I dreamt delirious dreams before a doctor diagnosed it properly and put me on antibiotics.

Sometime in that year, I also came across the next major spiritual influence in my life—a guru from Australia, called Barry Long.

Barry Long was in many ways a perfect antidote to Rajneesh—straight talking, very practical and with an ability to cut through a lot of the mystique with clear, down-to-earth suggestions. He was acknowledged by his followers—although he would have abhorred that term—as an enlightened master. He said he had 'passed through the illusion of death' during his own retreat to the Himalayas looking for truth.

Despite having realised truth in India, he had little time for the ritual and worshipful communities around Indian gurus or Tibetan masters. For a while, he was guru to Eckhart Tolle, who went on to become much better known but who acknowledged Barry Long's influence on an Oprah Winfrey appearance!

I first heard Barry Long speak in London and was impressed by both his logic and also his perspective on man-woman relationships. He spoke to the ex-Rajneeshees who were in the audience and told them their approach to sex was self-indulgent and causing them too much confusion. His teaching included very specific instructions for transforming sex within a committed relationship and for addressing the areas where self-delusion reigns.

I had sometimes experienced making love as more than a physical and emotional thing—that it can be the most real and spiritual thing; a doorway to the timeless. I had also experienced the potential for devastating confusion and pain in my relationships. I was eager to work consciously with Barry Long's approach but it had come too late for my relationship with Ellis, and Chandragiri was also starting to slip beyond my reach while he grappled with other challenges.

6

WORLD TURNED UPSIDE DOWN

I ENROLLED FOR A WEEKEND SEMINAR with Barry Long in Regent's Park in London and, by the end of it, found myself in a calmly blissful state I hadn't known since Poona. This feeling was always one of coming home and greater reality, rather than an escape from reality. From this state, it seemed clear that mental noise and the business of living were normally obscuring the awareness of being totally connected to the perfection, wonder and beauty of life.

Barry Long also spoke of 'Being' as preferable to meditation—a vital distinction that focuses on a state of inner and outer awareness simultaneously. It is a state of full awareness, which is also our natural state before self-consideration and thought arises. Meditation is simply a useful tool to still the mind so we can return to Being.

In some ways, Barry's teaching, and that of most mystics, aligns with contemporary science in saying the mind is mechanical. But, unlike scientists who continue to listen to the mechanical mind as the sole source of their knowledge, the spiritual path tries to still the mind to experience or merge with what is beyond.

In Barry's words:

> *Your robot mind is the problem. It will not stay still and you cannot make it stay still. It is your master and it separates you from beauty and God. To experience you exist, the mind is momentarily stopped. You draw all your faculties into yourself, you meditate on the moment and you experience 'I am'... If you could hold that state, even the 'I am' would disappear and you would be in the silence on the edge of time. For this split second, you are at the apex of consciousness; just beyond is where God, the timeless or the uncreated begins.*

In his very practical way, Barry also discouraged any insubstantial systems of esoteric thought. He said that anything we can see is not God. Anything we can think is not God. Neither are visions, lights, moving objects or anything else. Any sensation or feeling is not God. They are all products of the creation or our imagination.[8]

The scientists would doubtless agree with him on that one.

On a personal level, the new teaching didn't protect me from pain and confusion but it did give a thin thread to hold onto through some of the dark days to come.

I didn't know how or where to pick up the pieces of my life. The hurt of separation reappeared in any quiet moments, which made meditation more difficult. Ellis and I had sold our joint home and I had bought a small townhouse without a garden. Lily spent alternate weeks with me and Ellis.

So here I was, still in grey England, now without a partner, and feeling as if I'd been bowled over by a tsunami. Watching clothes going around in the launderette, depression descended and I wondered where I'd gone wrong.

The only thing I knew that might shift things for me was travel. I decided I needed an adventure before Lily got to school age, when we'd be more tied to one place. I used some money put aside from the house sale to book a round-the-world ticket.

We spent a few months wandering through Thailand and Malaysia. I loved the adventure and the stimulation of each day being fresh and unexpected—sometimes not unexpected in a good way but that was all part of the challenge. Despite the new vistas, there were some evenings, after Lily had gone to bed in our Thai beach bungalow, that I gazed out over the ocean and feel like howling at the moon—for love, for contentment, for I knew not what.

Next stop was Australia, where the air was fresh, light and stunningly bright after the heavy humidity of Thailand. In Western Australia, we headed for Fremantle where I knew there was a *sannyasin* community and we rented a room there. One of the other rooms was rented by Sam, a lovely *sannyasin* man who played sublime guitar, played cricket with Lily in the garden and cooked vegetarian dinners for all of us.

Wise people would say it was way too soon after two major relationship break-ups to embark on another one but I was never wise in that way. We had been thrown together, almost like an instant family while the house owner was away in India, and we were having fun together.

Before long, I went to his room in the evenings while Lily slept and sneaked back to my own bed next to hers before she woke.

I initially considered it to be a holiday romance, with enjoyable times as we all sang along to the Travelling Wilburys in the car or watched shooting stars over the water somewhere along the south-west coast. Then it got more serious when it was time for us to leave. Did it have to end?

There was a pivotal moment when I'd met a little Australian girl on her bike in the back streets of Fremantle and felt a compelling desire to bring Lily up in Australia where the sun was shining and people were smiling; where there was a certain innocence in the kids and endless space for them to play. I'd also seen Barry Long speaking in Perth and wondered if my next life-stage lay here where I could have regular contact with him.

It was one of my enduring delusions to imagine life was leading me to something I wanted and that somehow that would result in the best outcomes for all. If life was leading me anywhere, it was along a painful road of getting more detached from my wants and the things that I thought I needed for my happiness! Later I questioned whether we are ever in control of anything, even our own thoughts and actions—but more of that later.

Going with the flow, this lovely but quite troubled man followed me to USA, where I visited old *sannyasin* friends, and then to England.

The warning signs were there even in the early days of that relationship, as we settled back for a winter in England, but I thought we could get over the difficulties together.

After a few months and a violent outburst against me, Sam admitted to an alcohol problem. He said he was keen to get help and start afresh.

My optimism and seeing the potential in people triumphed over evidence. I agreed to marry him so we would have the freedom to continue the relationship without visa hassles. I loved his positive side and his keenness to try the Barry Long approach to a relationship. I hoped we might make a good life together in Australia.

Although the seed of promise of a better way of life had been planted during my visit to Australia, the soul-searching of the decision to emigrate was considerable. There seemed to be nothing for me in England and it was hard to make ends meet. I continued to dream of a life in the sun somewhere but I knew I would be hurting Ellis and compounding the effect of our separation by taking Lily so far away. I would also be leaving my sister, brother, parents and friends. I felt guilty for wanting to leave but it felt like something I simply had to do. In my growing enthusiasm for the new possibilities, I minimised the potential long-term problems—for everyone including myself.

In late 1990, we moved to Australia. From the perspective of my spiritual exploration, the important point is that I ended up living at Tamborine Mountain in Queensland, about 25 kilometres from where Barry Long held monthly meetings. These Sunday afternoon sessions were a source of guidance for the next seven or eight years.

Like Rajneesh, Barry Long was a charismatic spontaneous speaker but, with a relatively small number of attendees at each meeting—perhaps 100-150—it was always possible to ask questions and have an intelligent dialogue as well as to learn from other people's questions.

He contended that the Eastern masters couldn't teach the west because the cultural background was so different. He said that, as an ordinary man who'd earned his living in Sydney and London, who'd been through many of the typical experiences of contemporary life—marriage, divorce, death of a loved one—he was able to 'keep us honest'.

He cautioned that while the Eastern traditions have much of truth to offer, the west gets caught in the ritual and makes a lifestyle of it all, which tends to enforce the idea of self rather than diminish it. I knew from experience that some of the people who put on *sannyasin* robes and changed their name had developed a spiritual arrogance and inflated sense of their self-importance and holiness.

Above all, he tried to demonstrate simple truths 'in our own experience'. He said the only things worth speaking of were beauty, truth, death, love and God but that they weren't things to be 'discussed' as a social chat with friends. He constantly urged people to test what he said and not to simply believe. He spoke of God not as a personal God; more as the substratum and intelligence of existence—Life with a capital 'L'.

He also continually clarified the difference between the

body-mind that will eventually die and the 'I' that is the pure consciousness. He often spoke from that 'I', much as Krishna does in the *Bhagavad Gita* or Jesus does in the Bible—but then he immediately said, "Remember there is only one I in the universe and it's sitting on that chair".

From this perspective, when Jesus says, "I and the father are one" or "before Abraham was born, I am!", or Krishna in the Bhagavad Gita says, "I am the seed of all things that are; and no being that moves or moves not can ever be without me", they are speaking from the shared place of eternity in each of us, which we can know beyond the busy mind and ideas of what we think we are.

Barry's teaching was not only a theoretical paradigm but also very much a way-of-living. One of his important lessons for me, as a very emotional person, was not to follow my fluctuating feelings but to look for the deeper knowledge beneath.

> *Feelings are constantly changing. None is dependable for long. You can love someone intensely today, and tomorrow or next month not feel a thing. Except perhaps for the feeling of doubt or depression that what was so beautiful could change so quickly.*[9]

He spoke of love not as a feeling that can come and go but as an unchanging state. He said that certain people may reflect that unchanging love to us but they are not the cause of it. People may come and go but love always exists within us.

This was a vital touchstone for me over the coming years, not least because Sam turned out to be a man facing far more persistent demons than I'd imagined and our relationship was on-again, off-again for quite a few years. We tried to live Barry's teaching but struggled with the challenges of everyday life.

I know I was obstinate in some ways, putting Lily's needs first in refusing to shift from the school where she was settled so he could move somewhere that work would be easier to find. In an unpredictable relationship, it became important to cling to what was working for us—and I loved seeing Lily flower in the positive environment of Tamborine Mountain where we were living.

Our first break-up was only six months after we arrived in Australia and, suddenly, I was a sole parent managing on my own in a country where I had no family or close friends to call on. I had only spasmodic freelance income and the emotional ups and downs had taken their toll. Although I collapsed in an emotional heap many times, I loved Australia and was doggedly determined to make our lives work here.

The marriage reunited on a few hopeful occasions to try afresh. In the best times, we enjoyed our everyday life, often with joy in making music, creating art or playing with the cats in the garden—but always tensions got too much and we had to call 'time out'. When Sam played guitar to accompany Lily composing on her electronic keyboard, or helped her record a Christmas cassette tape to send to England, or when he took her out to spot possums by torchlight, my heart relaxed but another storm cloud was always over the horizon.

In the meantime, Ellis arrived to see Lily at least once a year or, as she got a little older, she flew back to visit him for Christmas. Some years, she also visited the family with me in the English summertime. Early on, Ellis even tried to get residency in Australia and was sponsored for a position in Sydney for a while but that didn't work out for him and my idea that we might all manage to stay close in Australia and all have a better life turned out to have been another case of wishful thinking.

With his return to England, he seemed to be fading from my life and I knew I was more alone than ever.

Lily's primary school years were both enjoyable and very demanding. Without much work, we had little money but there were many childhood milestones to celebrate and I never doubted that her life in Australia was better than it would have been in England. Tamborine Mountain was a small slice of paradise and I felt that she was having an idyllic small-community upbringing with many school friends. A couple who had also moved from England to Queensland at the same time as us to be close to Barry were a source of like-minded friendship for me. Slowly we built a small circle of people with whom we could share a meal or conversation.

In the winter, I collected wood for the pot-belly stove and, in the summer, we went to the beach. I walked most days in the rainforest and did the usual 'school mum' things.

We moved home five times as we could only afford to rent and often landlords decided to sell or move back into their own homes, forcing us to move on. From one perspective, we were gypsies with a tenuous hold on a sense of belonging but the natural surroundings, space and sunshine were ongoing inspiration that held me to the Australian environment.

In addition to occasional freelance work, I started writing children's and young adult novels. They were all set in Queensland and drew on local places, describing the sub-tropical landscapes that surrounded me. After the books were published, I was invited to many country and bush towns, running writing workshops for schools and finding new satisfaction in being a rambling author on tour.

One winter's evening, when my erratic Australian marriage seemed finally over and I was playing on the new-fangled internet, I tried to trace Chandragiri, who I hadn't heard from for a quite a few years. I knew he'd gone to Cambodia and wondered if he was still okay. He was an only child, whose parents had died when he was in his early twenties, so there was no-one to check if he was alive or dead there.

I eventually managed to trace him through the British Embassy there and he was delighted to hear from me. He had recently split up from his partner and was really keen to visit me. I wondered if perhaps that was a sign that we would reunite. Was he the one I should have been with all along?

Perhaps my life has been a litany of hope outstripping realism—certainly I've had an optimism that is rarely borne out by events!

Chandragiri had only been at my place a few hours when he was going cold turkey from a heroin addiction that I knew nothing about. He stumbled around the house, hardly knowing where he was, shivering and shaking, slobbering and occasionally wailing.

I was torn between anger that he'd dumped this on me and deep concern for him. I phoned helplines and friends but there seemed to be nothing I could do but let him go through it. Thankfully, Lily was staying with friends and wasn't subjected to this frightening drama.

After a few days, he was calm and we had many conversations, catching up on the things we'd been doing. He was suffering from a relationship break-up—the Canadian woman he'd been with in Cambodia who had shared his addiction had recently been rescued by her parents and hadn't been heard from again.

There was still a way in which he transformed the mundane for me and made me feel delight in life. For all my life experience, I still don't know what that alchemy was. I took him for a long drive through the beautiful countryside near Tamborine Mountain. From time to time he dozed, as he was still recovering from cold turkey but, whenever I looked in his direction, I felt a timeless connection; that we had always been together.

We drove with Lily, now a young teenager, and one of her friends down to Byron Bay, for a short holiday. Chandragiri loved Byron Bay and got a small tattoo to remind him of this time there. We met up with a woman-friend of mine and walked in the rainforest at Springbrook. Later that evening, we came across a guy with a telescope in a pub garden who showed us the stars. It felt as if there was always potential for magical situations when Chandragiri was around.

His intense (perhaps bi-polar) personality was hard work though and, in some ways, I breathed a sigh of relief when it was time for him to return to Cambodia. It might have been different if he wasn't reeling from his broken love affair but I think he'd long ago filed me under 'f' for friend, although he acknowledged how special our relationship had been.

Later he returned to England, got clean from the heroin and we met up for a coffee and conversation whenever I was back there for a visit. Sometimes we'd walk and talk—on Brighton's pier or on the Sussex Downs—and time always seemed to stand still for a while.

Barry Long's wisdom continued to be a beacon to keep me on some sort of track. Although he was sometimes very forthright and authoritative in responding to people, he also showed great compassion. Speaking to a mother whose child had died, he acknowledged the tremendous grief and gave time for tears but delivered a truth no-one else might dare to. As he said in an interview:

> *People have been suffering since time began, losing their jobs and their lives and their children because that's living, isn't it? And you must deal with it. Not worry and think and try to work it out. Not ask why did this happen, but rather see there must be something I have to learn here. Then instead of blaming and wondering and speculating, I can discover the truth that everybody dies, that everything changes every moment.*[10]

He goes on to say that no creature is safe, nothing is

guaranteed and eventually we have to face the fact that, "My God, I can hold on to nothing. I can be attached to nothing. And yet I can enjoy what I have. And if it goes, as it must go, then I'm no longer shocked because I know that I can't hold on to anything, including my own life".

As if to prove that transience, in 1999 I had a particularly bad year.

7

THE END OF MY TETHER

THE DUST HAD LONG SETTLED on Chandragiri's visit and a divorce from Sam was in process. Lily was 15 and we both felt it would be a good time to move to Brisbane where the city would offer broader school subject choices for her final years, as well as more job opportunities for me.

Perhaps I allowed myself a little self-congratulation at having got through hard times and still been a good mother to Lily. I took delight in the fact that she was thriving. At 15 she was confident, had good friends, was one of the top academic performers at her school, was a Gold Coast debating champion, a good swimmer, a competent netballer and was pretty well-balanced despite one or two typical teenage moments.

I also entertained the possibility that maybe now my life experience had taught me enough that I could finally be a good partner to Ellis. I was confident we would get things right now—better late than never. I hoped he would like to live with us in Brisbane. I knew he hadn't much liked Tamborine Mountain but this would be a fresh start for all of us.

I'd had plenty of exciting times and I didn't need that sort of stimulation anymore. My soul was yearning for the man with stability, the man who really understood me, the dear friend who had always been there with a sweet heart—and I imagined I could heal the past for all of us. I also felt I had so much more love, more understanding and more stability to bring to the relationship myself since absorbing the Barry Long teachings.

I imagined Ellis would be as happy as I was with this plan as he had always said I was 'the one' and he hadn't had any lasting relationships since our separation. I wanted to commit myself to making him happy after all the ups and downs of the past. Perhaps we would even marry and find ourselves together on that park bench in old age as I had imagined so many years ago!

The house-move turned out to be disastrous. Perhaps I was exhausted from the past ten years, the move from the mountain and suffering from menopause but everything seemed wrong about the new place, from the stained shag-carpets to the crumbling, chipboard, bathroom cabinets. Lily had gone to England for Christmas with Ellis and I felt desperately lonely and wanted to be with the two of them.

When I told Ellis of my renewed hope for us, I discovered that he had a serious new love interest after all these years and that I had been living in a dream world with my thoughts of a happy reunion.

I was devastated. Life seems so cruel sometimes and I had struggled so long to create some elusive perfect life. My belief that if you do your best and follow your heart, things will turn out happily for everyone in the end, was deeply shaken, if not destroyed.

It turned out that the move to Brisbane was also disastrous for Lily. She hated her new school from day I and felt that she would never achieve her academic goals in that environment. With all of that year counting towards her final score for university entrance, it wasn't a time to get things wrong. A wiser mother might have been a steadying influence and insisted she stay for a term at least but I was past knowing what was the right thing for us. It's possible the outcomes to that would have been even worse anyway.

We checked out alternative schools in Brisbane and eventually decided maybe the whole move had been ill-advised and we should return to Tamborine Mountain for her to finish school there. Her old school warmly accepted her back but there was another problem. I couldn't find us a good place to rent back on the mountain.

As a result, Lily stayed with a friend on the mountain during the week but the friends' parents were going through divorce and things were not easy for her staying there. Being away from home and feeling guilty that she had upset our move to Brisbane may have contributed to her developing anorexia.

To start with, I had no real idea how bad anorexia could be but as weeks passed things became desperate and anorexia was the central focus in our lives.

During the second term, we gave up on her arrangement of staying with friends and she travelled each day. I drove the 90 minutes each way once a day, occasionally twice. Other days, she got a train one way as far as it went and a taxi up the mountain—thanks to Ellis subsidising the cost.

By mid-year, she was too weak to take the train—her weight-loss meant people were knocking her over on the platform. I now needed to take her to school and collect her. After another few weeks, she was confined to home, painfully thin and obviously suffering her own deep anguish. My daughter was disappearing in front of my eyes.

We drove the length and breadth of Brisbane to specialist doctors and psychologists trying to find an answer.

Anorexia is like an intense addiction. It is virtually impossible for the sufferer to break the physical-mental cycle once it is established—the low food intake creates physiological changes that trigger the brain's obsessive thinking. Logic, encouragement, inducement or threats are all useless, although that doesn't stop a desperate mother thinking that she might be able to talk her child into eating something.

More weeks passed and nothing was working. We were days away from Lily being hospitalised and were warned it wouldn't be pretty. She would be force-fed in a mental ward. The prognosis wasn't good. Death was a possibility.

Somehow, weak and anguished, Lily struggled with herself and pulled herself back from the brink. The psychologist had said she must drink Sustagen during the next few days to keep herself out of hospital. The next morning, she came into my bedroom early and asked me if she could have a piece of toast instead of Sustagen. I hugged her bony, cold body and said of course. It was the first solid food she had eaten for many weeks.

We had turned a corner but every meal was a mountain for her to traverse. Calories and fat were enemies to be encountered and negotiated before anything could be consumed.

As she slowly recovered, Ellis visited. I looked to him for some loving interaction to heal the pain of our daughter's desperate time but he was pretty much beyond reach—practical and concerned for the short time he was there but distant and detached. My response was not always grateful or graceful. It all seemed so unfair and I was yearning for the family life and love I'd left behind.

I think most of us manage to rise to the occasion and cope through a crisis but the strain of it all hits us like a Mack truck when the worst of it is over. I was mentally and physically exhausted by the time Lily was properly on the road to recovery and back at school. I marched onwards but I felt as if the heart had been sucked out of me.

While all this was going on, there was a new friend, Jamie, who I knew was interested in me. His friendship and support were my only lifelines through this bleak period and we were both equally earnest about our 'spiritual development' but I couldn't fully reciprocate his desire for a relationship for a long time. Partly I didn't see him as 'my type' and partly I was still reeling from too much previous relationship confusion.

Early the next year, we agreed that, although we weren't together, we both felt guilty if we thought about seeing someone else. My choices had turned out to be pretty disastrous over the years so perhaps it would work to let someone choose me for a change. Perhaps I should surrender to a good man and valued friend who cared about me.

In truth, I also desperately needed some support. I had carried too much weight alone for too long. I didn't have the highest expectations for the relationship (perhaps a good thing) but I was willing to see where it wanted to lead us.

Where it led is another story with its times of loving togetherness and times when we took wrong turns. In Jamie, I had found a guardian angel who would be part of my life far longer than men I had pursued with more compelling certainty.

Lily recovered and returned to school for Year 12. She took driving lessons and passed her driving test. Ellis bought her a small second-hand car for her birthday so she could drive herself to school each day.

Before the end of that final school year, she crashed the car into a tree on her way back down the mountain. The car opened up like a sardine-can down the driver's side and was a write-off but I was more concerned that she had escaped with her life. She only had a scratch or two and a scattering of windscreen glass in her underwear.

Or did she? I sometimes wonder if that accident and the anorexia period were the end of her belief that life was a safe place and she could always cope with it all.

Ellis was angry and seemed to draw even further away from both of us. From a distance, it seemed as if he cared more about the lost car money than the trauma we'd gone through. All the car-money was gone because I was living hand-to-mouth with minimum funds and hadn't been able to afford the high cost of fully-comprehensive insurance for a teenager. It's possible he was frustrated at watching us lurch from one catastrophe to the next.

We pulled the threads back together yet again and all would have looked pretty good on the surface at the end of that year. Lily had been school captain and was dux of the school at her graduation. She had a high score for university entrance, despite having missed more than a term of Year 11 and she was accepted into the University of Queensland. She set off on a post-school trip to USA, Italy and UK to visit friends and family.

Despite having a new man in my life, I was struggling to make sense of everything that had happened. After eight house moves in a bit over a decade and struggling to hold everything together for so long, I was exhausted.

I'd followed the trail of love but somehow ended up losing love every time. Worst of all, I felt I had lost touch with the deeper spiritual reality again over the past couple of years while grappling with all the concerns, emotions and worries of living.

I'd made what I thought were many courageous choices in good faith through my life but I'd ended up weaker and poorer. Perhaps this was bad karma and I should never have left Ellis way back in those days when everything seemed stuck. Perhaps I'd inflicted so much pain that this was what I had reaped.

I reached a crisis point where I felt that all of my searching and spiritual effort had been wasted. I was no better able to deal with life or stay attuned to a deeper reality than I had been 20 years before. What's more, I had focused on the spiritual life rather than the material one and had nothing to show for it. I'd hurt people I loved, I'd loved people who weren't able to reciprocate and I'd ended up with no money and no enduring wisdom.

My resilience had reached its breaking point.

I wrote to Barry Long in anguish, told him of my troubles and said I had been on the spiritual path for all this time but I didn't feel I was getting anywhere. What more could I do? What did it take? And how long?

His reply was basically 'There is no path. There is only now'. It wasn't what I wanted to hear and I pushed the letter away, disgusted. Ungrateful student that I was, I didn't even keep the letter but no doubt it reflected what he said here in a 1988 talk:

> *There is no path to God or truth. Everyone is counting on the future, is working towards some purity. And it does not exist. The only impediment to your realising this truth is that you think there is a spiritual path. You think there is a way to God, to truth, to self-realisation. All that is a lie. And as long as you practise it, think about it, follow it, participate in it, you are living a lie to yourself...*

He goes on to say that, while we think there is a spiritual path, we are not facing 'now' and that in imagining a better tomorrow we are preventing ourselves from being the truth now.

When I boiled down all I had heard, read, learnt and experienced, there seemed to be nothing to hold on to. I was still sinking beneath life's pressures. I was falling apart. My life was a mess. I decided my spiritual search was over. The only logical truth I knew was to be present and experience each moment. Whether there was a God or not, a soul or not, or a purpose or not, I might as well make the most of every moment by staying right here and not letting thoughts move to past or future.

It felt as if my life was over, the pain was unbearable and I might as well die. What happened next took me by surprise.

8

A SURPRISE GLIMPSE

WITHIN DAYS OF GIVING UP, something shifted. Fragmented bits of world became a perfect whole.

Everywhere I looked, there was a sense of beauty, perfection, rightness, unity. The peace and depth behind the physical world felt eternal and unchanging—much more real than the shifting patterns of life on the surface. I was seeing God everywhere—not a vision of a personal God but an almost visible vibrancy and clarity in everything. The person looking was more like a mirror than an active instrument—a tiny part of the picture but also containing the whole.

There was no need to be in a quiet or peaceful place to see this reality—it was there as much in the busy shopping mall as in the forest, as much in a table as in a flower. I felt a loving connection with everyone without cultivating any particular attitude or trying to see the divine in them.

The world was an incredible, beautiful dance supported by and infused with an eternally unchanging principle and mystery that could be felt but never described. It was certainly not a mystery to be solved—it was a mystery to be known and to merge into, not that I had ever been separate from it for a moment, even when I thought I had.

I saw the space between things, not the solidity, lived in the silence that contains the sound.

From time to time, the Muslim phrase '*La ilaha il Allah*' (there is no god but God) broke the stillness of my mind. I only knew it from a Sufi group in Poona days but its melodic acknowledgement of the primacy of God seemed appropriate and gave the mind a means to express what was inexpressible.

Sometimes riding on the back of Jamie's motorbike, and later on my own motorbike, there was a feeling of flowing as part of all that is. The separate 'me' was a thin membrane on the whole vibrant, pulsating reality.

This changed perception persisted at different levels of intensity for a few months and then seemed to retreat again.

The focus on the personal life is a very old habit attached to the body and, in time, it reformed in patches. Since then though, the solid idea of 'Julia' has never been quite such a permanent and believable fixture—more a passing phantom that forgets it's a phantom for short periods. It's an identification with the role I'm playing; much like an actor believing for a short while that they are a character they are portraying.

The knowledge of that time is still contained in this body-mind—the memory gives a lasting perspective and an underlying orientation to life but it is very different from the living experience of those few months.

Unless one is part of a monastic order, and probably even then, mundane life demands continue to intervene and at times it seems as if that is the only reality.

Life went on. I moved in with Jamie and we got off to a pretty rocky start with our respective offspring and noisy neighbours adding additional layers of complication. Lily decided to stay in the UK to be with a man she'd met.

Not too long afterwards, my mother died. I flew back for her funeral, remembering a courageous woman who had spent her last thirty years in a wheelchair but who had always had faith in God and time to nurture friends and family.

I returned to full-time work for a while and now had no particular spiritual guidance or practice, except for coming back to Being and presence between busy times.

I look back on that time of changed perception as a turning point. Not a solution. Not an end to all problems. But as a total giving-up, at least temporarily, of the trying, doing self that thinks it is going to create something better—tomorrow, next week, next year.

Although some people manage to get all the pieces of their physical life lined up, in my experience, the happy equilibrium of circumstances is only ever fleeting.

Many people think a new partner, a new career, a diet, a boob job, a better house or more money might be the answer.

For those who have embraced a so-called spiritual life, it is one more book or workshop needed, or a few tweaks to attitude, to live a fulfilling and abundant life, find a soul mate and attract never-ending positivity and bliss.

My insight at that time turned such notions of self-improvement on their head. It's not self-improvement we need. It's self-transparency.

In my earlier years of 'searching' I had been approaching the quest as one approaches any worldly task. There was Julia and there was a world and perhaps there was also God or enlightenment that could be found through hints in old books or travelling to distant mountains! Like the knights of old, if I braved all the challenges along the way, I might eventually approach some heavily-guarded tower where the treasure lies within. It was a mystical hide-and-seek and I was very much the seeker.

Sitting at the feet of gurus, there was an unquestioned division between me and them. They had something I wanted and perhaps they could tell me how to get it or help me see it through a blast of their super-human energy. Sometimes I did imbibe something of the mystery but it was fleeting and I continued to look for the mechanisms to get more of it!

Inevitably I was introduced to the concept of 'ego' and how ego gets in the way. At that point I split the self-concept into a worthy, seeking Julia who is being thwarted by a part of herself called ego.

This message confused me and I think it confuses many people because they equate ego with a big sense of self-importance. They see themselves as a 'self' who has a big ego and who could be humble or modest with additional work and awareness. This is a cue to put on a spiritual or humble demeanour only to get caught in a loop of feeling a little superior because one is more restrained and not displaying a big ego!

If one is aware enough to catch the irony, one feels a little guilty and tries harder to be genuinely humble or to wallop the self-satisfied thought when it appears, much as one tries to wallop one of those 'moles' that rockets from a tube in a traditional fairground game!

Similarly, 'thinking' was an enemy and a further split emerged between me and the thoughts that had to be tamed.

These sorts of psychological games go on in anyone who tries to better themselves and much of the Mind Body Spirit movement is one of self-improvement.

The many books of guru and disciple dialogues on my shelves have hundreds of seekers over the years asking 'What should I do to get there?', 'How do I deal with this aspect of me that is a barrier?', 'What sort of meditation should I do?', 'How do I stop the mind from getting in the way?'.

With the few months of clarity in this body-mind organism when the Julia-person gave up, it started to dawn that this 'self' is the problem. This concept of an individual being that must jump through certain hoops—stop doing this, do more of that—to get a yummy state of enlightenment or God-realisation is the barrier itself.

Philosophers, gurus have long been asking the question 'What is this self?' but I had been more concerned with 'What should this self be doing to find what it's looking for?'

Although there are places in the spiritual texts that make this clear, they reeked of the self-denial and martyrdom view of spirituality that I'd left behind in Catholicism and I didn't hear what they were actually trying to say.

In Evelyn Underhill's seminal work *Mysticism,* first published in 1910, Underhill concluded that, "All the mystics agree that the stripping off of the I, the Me, the Mine …is an imperative condition of the attainment of the unitive life".[11]

The ancient Indian *Kaushitaki Upanishad* says, "It is not mind which we should want to know: we should know the thinker".[12]

One of Indian's most revered 20th century sages, Ramana Maharshi, focused on this fundamental question, instructing questioners in a method of self-inquiry that is encapsulated in the phrase 'Who am I?'. The core teaching of his teaching was: "Whence does the 'I' arise? Seek this within. The 'I' then vanishes. This is the pursuit of wisdom".

John, my college friend, gave me a small Ramana Maharshi book[13] very early in my wanderings but I couldn't get what he was saying then. I wanted instructions on how to live and how to find God not a riddle about 'Who am I?'

Anthony De Mello, a Jesuit and director of the Sadhana Institute of Pastoral Counselling in Poona, before his death in 1987, said, "Most people, even though they don't know it, are asleep. They're born asleep, they live asleep, they marry in their sleep, they breed children in their sleep and they die in their sleep without ever waking up".

He had a similar message to Ramana Maharshi: "Who is the person doing the understanding? Find that out first. That's the foundation of everything, isn't it? It's because we haven't understood that we've got all these stupid religious people involved in all these stupid religious wars."[14]

Tibetan Lama, Chögyam Trungpa agrees that the self-idea is the problem:

> *The heart of the confusion is that man has a sense of self that seems to him to be continuous and solid. When a thought or emotion or event occurs, there is a sense of someone being conscious of what is happening. You sense that you are reading these words. This sense of self is actually a transitory, discontinuous event, which in our confusion seems to be quite solid and continuous.*[15]

He says that, because we take our confused view as reality, we are always struggling to maintain and enhance this solid self. We spend our lives trying to feed it pleasure and shield it from pain. He repeats the Buddha's teaching that we are seduced by a fundamental myth—that we are solid beings. "But ultimately the myth is false, a huge hoax, a gigantic fraud and is the root of our suffering."

My Australian guru, Barry Long, also said that our sense of self is an illusory construction reinforced by memory, "Through the feeling of having been, we get the feeling of being someone, something. It is a substitute for being now. It is comforting, reassuring almost to the point of necessity for most of us; but it is not the truth. To be someone or something at any time requires living in the past".

I remember a time when Barry Long asked us to stop telling our story, and especially our 'sad story'.

While I see now how telling that story can reinforce a solid (and illusory) sense of self, at the time it felt like a huge loss. How would anyone know me without my story? I might as well have done nothing in my life if I couldn't share it. In truth, I thought of myself as a package of feelings, memories and choices. Part of that package was physical but a larger part was the experiences, adventures and challenges that made me who I am.

Like a lot of spiritual practices, this exercise was intended to shine a light on something and was not intended to be a code of conduct or a commandment to make us more worthy of divine approval. Sometimes it's difficult to tell the difference when hearing guidance from someone who has learned a little more of life.

After Barry's exercise, I was definitely more reluctant to tell my personal story. But I was still very much a self who *was not* telling its story rather than a self who *was* telling its story!

With the shift in my consciousness when the self gave up, I started to see that the storyteller could go on living and doing whatever it did without feeling that I was intrinsically that.

The shift hadn't given me all the answers but I was seeing everything from a totally fresh perspective.

PART TWO

EXPLORING NON-DUALITY

9

LIVING WITHOUT MYSELF

AT THIS POINT THE STORY CHANGES. It is less about a personal journey because the person has become more transparent. And yet there is still a body-mind with memories floating around, with its preferences, with a tendency to avoid pain and to protect those it loves.

Not least of all, it prefers a decent roof over its head and has to earn a living to make that happen!

To operate in the world, it has to continue to play the original game of being a person but there is a dual-perception: Julia as a woman interacting spontaneously with the environment—and having thoughts of all sorts, though less of them—and an underlying knowledge that 'I am not that', or not entirely that.

Instead of being totally at the mercy of emotions and changing fortunes, most of the time I sense my roots in something deeper, in a place beyond self.

There is nothing to defend from criticism or to be built

up by praise, although acknowledgement and love continue to be sweet moments of connection with other humans—sweeter than ever because they resonate in presence rather than being grappled into a self-image.

After the months of revelation, I remained fascinated with how this no-self state and the sense of God are connected. And I felt strongly that the vocal atheist scientists are barking up the wrong tree with their dense materialism. They are the opposite polarity from the blind believers in a father figure in the sky—both sides seem equally stuck in a dogma.

The truth, I was sure, is infinitely richer and more mysterious, whether you approach it scientifically or through the metaphors of world religions.

I returned to familiar texts and researched new sources that might help give a more coherent view to satisfy the logical mind. After all, proclaiming "Julia doesn't exist and God is everywhere!" was likely to have me locked up or medicated unless I could also explain a bit better what it was all about!

To start with, I was drawn to books that explored the concept of self and what exactly a person is.

For most people, the self as we live it, know it and talk about it is never questioned. A bundle of memories, predispositions and awareness in a physical body has a name and has become a 'thing' that needs to be protected, analysed, worked on and promoted.

In fact, in recent times, the focus on self has increased, supported over the past decade with online forums for any self that wants to say something or share something—often an idealised version of itself packaged to inspire other selves to be better selves! To have 15 minutes—or even five—of fame, validates this self's existence for many. Carefully cultivating a self-image has reached new heights on social media channels like Instagram.

For the average person, the focus on 'my uniqueness', 'my individuality' and 'my self-interest' has probably never been more clearly differentiated and nurtured.

Self-esteem, self-confidence and even self-love are highly regarded and have almost become a cult. In certain psychological sectors, there's a belief that you can't love or serve another unless you love yourself first.

The flip side of all that is when one judges oneself to be inadequate, which often leads to shame, guilt, depression, self-hate and self-harm or a never-ending roller-coaster of self-improvement measures.

But who, or what, is this self that we're supposed to be loving and improving? And how much of what we assume is a self is an empty shared concept, a convenient metaphor for communication with other humans?

The conundrum of what we are has vexed philosophers for thousands of years and comes down to the mind-body-consciousness question.

The 'dualist' philosophers have always claimed the mind to have some sort of volition independent of the body—that the physical body is a tool directed by something else—but they have a major challenge in explaining the mechanisms by which this intangible thing could influence the body. Materialists are convinced that all we are, and all we see, is a collection of material interactions—full stop. 'Idealists' see a universe that is all immaterial or mentally constructed in some way.

Unless we are reared by wolves, none of us escapes the processes that build a sense of self.

Over 50 years ago Margaret Mahler, child development psychologist, said, "The infant's inner sensations form the core of the self. They seem to remain the central crystallisation point of the 'feeling of self' around which a 'sense of identity' will become established".[16]

Alison Gopnik, professor of psychology at University of California says, "We know that a child's conception of a continuous separate self develops slowly in the first five years... A single unified self is something we create—not something we are given".[17]

From a young age, when we start separating and naming things, we divide the world into multiple parts and start seeing the solidity of boundaries. In these early stages, we build the concept of a separate self on the distinction between 'me' and 'not-me'. Our parents reinforce that notion, we learn our name and, pretty soon, we start absorbing a barrage of commentary on whether we are good, bad, pretty, clever, cute or funny.

Are our parents and caregivers really teaching us what we are or are they creating an idea that will give us a solidity but has no basis in fact?

I remember when I was about 18, working in advertising but hankering after a career in journalism, I wrote an article for *Cosmopolitan*. It was an opinion-piece pointing out how we get stuck within the confines of description and of labels that we apply to ourselves and that others apply to us.

The article was rejected but I think perhaps it was an early intuition that what we are has nothing to do with those conceptual ideas, and that our opinions and self-definitions can be constantly changed, as long as we don't start believing in them.

What never occurred to me then is that even the core sense of self might be a conceptual construction. Although, I did sometimes feel that others had some solid sense of themselves that I had to fake. In a very subtle way, I felt I was acting what I wanted to be and not quite in touch with my own reality.

In recent years, neuroscience and evolutionary biology have come together to suggest that everything we are can be reduced to particular interactions of body activity, brain activity, environmental influences, DNA and genetic usefulness. There is no 'self' as an entity separate from that, they say.

Books such as *The Ego Tunnel* by Thomas Metzinger and *The Ego Trick* by Julian Baggini bring together recent neuroscience discoveries and philosophy to try to prove that our sense of self is an illusion.

Some of the most-quoted research in these books comes from V.S. Ramachandran's experiments. In these experiments, an amputee with a missing arm was positioned at a table with his remaining arm in a mirror box that reflected it and gave him the visual impression of two normal arms. The experimenter then stroked the normal arm, so it looked to the man as if both his arms were being stroked.

After a short time, he could experience sensations in his missing arm and also felt he could 'move' the non-existent limb.

Following on from these experiments, a rubber hand experiment showed that almost anyone could feel a sensation in a fake limb if one of his or her arms is hidden behind the back and replaced with a fake arm in a mirror box. As someone strokes both the real hand and the fake hand simultaneously, most people very soon experience sensation coming from the fake hand, even though their second real hand has not been touched.

To further demonstrate this, Metzinger, Olaf and Lenggenhager undertook experiments to try to get people to 'project' a sense of self into a virtual image. Some people did have a sense of shifting their identification somewhat, or feeling confused about the location of themselves—perhaps a bit like one might feel standing between opposing mirrors. This impression was less likely to happen if the virtual image was a wooden slab rather than a human figure.

Metzinger concludes that the fundamental sense of selfhood is found at the location of the visual body representation.

While, like many of us, I was happy to dismiss the physical body as a locus of self—after all, we know it changes over years and most parts can be replaced or enhanced these days—I had identified much more strongly with my thoughts and feelings.

Our responses seem unique and we are often illogically proud of them, if they are noble ones. We are happy to take credit for our courage, intelligent responses and loving actions, even if we feel we can take less credit for our 'lovely curly hair' or 'sexy bottom'. Equally we feel guilty for what we cannot achieve or when we fail those closest to us by our selfishness or lack of foresight.

Yet, how much of what we are is under our totally independent control? Psychologists and geneticists between them also lay claim to our intelligence levels, temperament and our likelihood of success or happiness.

We know mental illness and drugs like anti-depressants can change our perspective and relationship to the world, so even our feelings and mood are not something we can claim as an intrinsic and permanent element of who we are.

For most of us, although our body is an important part of self-concept and certainly an important aspect of self-promotion, we would probably say our self is something that lives *inside* the body. It's not only a physical sensation but a sense of a controller and integrator of the body's experience.

The scientists have claimed that's all the result of physical mechanisms too.

The discovery of mirror neurons has been used to argue that, even what we might consider some of our highest expressions of humanity—empathy and altruistic impulses—are the by-product of neurons that fire when we watch an action, in exactly the same way as they fire if we were performing the action ourselves.

In the 1980s and 1990s, neurophysiologists at the University of Palma in Italy started this ball rolling when they found that certain neurons in the monkey brain that fired when a monkey reached for food also fired when the monkey watched a person reach for food. We are wired to understand each other's experience.

Since then, there has been considerable research and controversy over the existence and role of mirror neurons in humans. While some argue that mirror neurons do not exist in humans, others have claimed an important role for them in human understanding and even a sense of self.

With all this evidence for our mechanical functioning, what is left? Our thoughts and decisions perhaps? Are they our own or only the result of genetic and childhood influences or random firing of neurons?

I was fascinated to discover that, in 2008, research with fMRIs showed movement in the brain as much as 10 seconds before the subject was conscious of making a decision.

Neuroscientists at the Max Planck Institute for Human Cognitive and Brain Sciences in Leipzig, Germany made fMRI images of the brains of volunteers while they performed a decision-making task.

The volunteers were asked to press one of two buttons at a random time of their choosing. Each button was operated by a different hand. At the same time, a stream of letters was presented on a screen and the volunteers had to remember which letter was showing when they decided to press the button.

Researchers were able to predict from brain activity which

hand would press the button *seconds before* the volunteer was even conscious of making a decision.

Commentators were quick to talk about the death of free will, although this could also be interpreted as proof of a more mysterious ground of our being that precedes the neurons lighting up the brain in a volitional action.

As brain research continues apace, my bookshelves have started to groan under the weight of different insights into the way we think and the different brain functions that integrate our perceptions or colour our shifting memories.

It looks as if we are not as autonomous as we'd like to believe. Yet our sense of being an independent doer persists and gives intrinsic meaning to the whole business of being alive.

We continue to cling to the idea of selfhood and it seems to cling to us. Despite philosophers and scientists deconstructing it, we continue to feel as if we are a continuous 'ghost in the machine'—a phrase introduced in philosopher Gilbert Ryle's book *The Concept of Mind* in 1949 to dispute Descartes dualist systems.

That 'inner person' is precious and responsible, hurt by disrespect, uplifted by praise, proud and ashamed in whatever balance seems appropriate.

If I fully believe in my 'self' as an entity and base that sense of self on my achievements, work, relationships or appearance, I am on shaky ground. If that sense of self takes a bitter blow or has its solidity shaken by a crisis of failure, rejection or lost reputation, different things can happen.

Some people sink into depression, swapping a trying-self for a not-worth-trying self. Some may even be tempted to take their own lives because a hopeless self or an anguished self without any other framework of meaning leaves an awful emptiness. Some may eventually patch up the self, using various forms of therapy and any positive thinking they can muster.

For me at the point of crisis, years of trying and failing to make progress on any of the fronts that mattered to me also left the 'self' in this body broken. Perhaps because I was in a state of mental and physical exhaustion as well as emotional pain, there was nothing to do but give up.

At first the vessel seemed empty but then, for a while, the space inside it simply merged with the space outside. Perhaps the years of meditation had left my brain better able to withstand the emptiness or perhaps that strange dissolution of self would have happened anyway.

10

BEYOND THE FILTER OF SELF

IT SEEMS TO ME THAT self-monitoring is like an endless movie or binge-watching a TV series. What is in front of me takes my full attention. It gives me rewarding feelings when the story goes the way I want and disappointed feelings when an obstacle gets in the way of happy outcomes.

At some point, when I turn off the TV or the credits roll, I realise it wasn't reality after all. Of course, with the personal self, it's much harder to find the 'off' button.

I am convinced that many of the religious practices through the ages have been attempts to hit that 'off' button.

Whether someone is praying many hours a day, meditating, chanting, sitting at the feet of a guru, devoting their life to service, practising ascetic penances, dancing to a trance state or going on a pilgrimage, they are setting aside the personal self and surrendering to something greater.

Of course, prayer and pilgrimage are used by some people purely to try to get a powerful God to intervene to achieve their personal or material wants but, for many, the objective is communion, union, *darshan* (seeing the divine) or *samadhi* (union with the divine) not only a supernatural shopping expedition.

The need to surrender is common to many paths of religious thought. The very name Islam actually means surrender.

This doesn't make sense for most of us in the contemporary individualistic west where we are busy creating our story of achievement and feathering our own nest. Surrender has negative connotations at this time in our culture. Instead, we are urged to boldly chase our dreams, to be our best self, to never give up.

Yet, what we are being asked to surrender was nothing substantial anyway. To surrender the 'me' or 'self' is simply to give up believing in a false idea.

While the end of a movie brings us back to the environment around us and the practical necessities of life, not many people have turned off the self to report what reality is beyond.

When that self is fully silenced for a period, they often report quite incredible things, hard to even express in words.

A meditation teacher quoted in Jack Kornfield's book *After the Ecstasy the Laundry* says:

> *Then somehow I let go further and entered the deepest peace imaginable, without even the subtlest sound or sensation… I didn't feel my body or mind at all, just pure consciousness. My whole identity dropped away. It was breathtaking, fantastic,*

> *beyond bliss. I knew I could never fear death after this because it is only this timeless, unborn consciousness that is real.*[18]

Swami Abishiktananda, who was born in France in 1910 as Henri Le Saux and later become a Benedictine monk, devoted his whole life to his Christian faith. After moving to India in 1948 to spread the Christian message, he encouraged a dialogue between Christianity and Hinduism and visited the revered guru Ramana Maharshi.

After years in India, he found his heart increasingly torn between the Roman Catholic liturgy and his realisations that went beyond the Christian orthodoxy. His dilemma was ultimately resolved in 1973 while he lay on the pavement in Rishikesh after a heart attack.

> *Really a door opened in heaven when I was lying on the pavement. But a heaven which was not the opposite of earth, something which was neither life nor death, but simply 'being', 'awakening'... beyond all myths and symbols. It is wonderful to pass through such an experience which makes you find full peace and happiness beyond all situations, even of death and life. Life cannot be the same anymore because beyond life we have found the Awakening.*[19]

About 100 years before I was investigating this phenomenon, William James (psychologist and brother of novelist Henry James), was collecting examples in his respected study *Varieties of Religious Experience,* originally published in 1902. Here is an example from a clergyman:

> *I remember the night, and almost the very spot on the hill-top, where my soul opened out, as it were, into the Infinite and there was a rushing together of the two worlds, the inner and the outer... I did not seek Him, but felt the perfect union of my spirit with His. The ordinary sense of things around me faded. For the moment nothing but an effable joy and exultation remained. It is impossible to fully describe the experience. It was like the effect of some great orchestra when all the separate notes have melted into one swelling harmony...*

William James also quotes a Dr. Bucke, a Canadian psychiatrist who experienced the following:

> *Directly afterward there came upon me a sense of exultation, of immense joyousness accompanied or immediately followed by an intellectual illumination impossible to describe. Among other things, I did not merely come to believe but I saw that the universe is not composed of dead matter, but is, on the contrary, a living Presence; I became conscious in myself of eternal life. It was not a conviction that I would have eternal life, but a consciousness that I possessed eternal life then; I saw that all men are immortal; that the cosmic order is such that without any peradventure all things work together for the good of each and all; that the foundation principle of the world, of all the worlds, is what we call love and that the happiness of each and all is in the long run absolutely certain.*[20]

While each person's description of a beyond-self state may be coloured by their beliefs and whether they have a theological background or not, there are many similarities.

Here's another one from Mani Bhaumik, one of the pioneers of laser technology used in corrective eye surgery. In *Code Name God,* he relates some of his early experiences as a boy in India which, although largely forgotten when he made a life of celebrity and fortune in USA, came to inspire a deeper perspective later in his life.

Walking with his father one night, at around age 10, he suddenly perceived the world differently:

> *A raven rose from the paddies, disturbed by our passage. As I followed the beating of the wings upward, I beheld the sky as never before, and my heart opened to receive it. The stars, I knew, I had always been there but on this night their infinitude overwhelmed me and flooded my consciousness with an indescribable feeling of unity.*

He asked his father, "Is this God?".

Another time he walked to the edge of the Ganges with his grandmother, climbed a high embankment and saw the glimmering expanse of water:

> *Once again, I felt the vastness before my eyes shift my awareness to another level altogether, to the sphere that I learned later in life was that of a genuine mystical experience. It was as if the consciousness of nature interpenetrated my own and found itself at home there.*[21]

It seems that the off-switch for the self and the merging

with a greater presence can be spontaneous—what may have been called 'grace' in the Christian tradition—and it can be cultivated by meditation, but often it is the result of emotional or physical crisis.

Eckhart Tolle, author of the popular book *Power of Now,* relates in his introduction how a deep depression and meaninglessness culminated in his thoughts stopping and new realisation:

> *I recognised the room and yet I knew I had never truly seen it before. Everything was fresh and pristine, as if it had just come into existence. I picked up things… marvelling at the beauty and aliveness of it all. That day I walked around the city in utter amazement at the miracle of life on earth, as if I had just been born into the world.*[22]

Barry Long too was in a place of extreme despair when he had a life-changing experience. In India and alone, after a relationship break-up and eight weeks of feeling he was about to die, he went through two days of confusion, uncertainty and lack of will.

> *On the third day I realised I was dead. Shortly after, I realised immortality. Death was a condition of the mind but it was not a fact. I had somehow passed through that condition. And now I was exultant, filled with the joy and knowledge that I was actually one with the life in nature, with every creature and living thing. I was forever, as life was. I was at peace. I was in no hurry to do anything, or not to do anything. I was choiceless. I was free.*[23]

While for some people going beyond the self is a blissful resolution to an agonising phase of emotional pain or searching, for others, the feeling is much more ambivalent.

I met a man called Laurie in Brisbane when I was working on this book. He said his sense of self was always fairly transparent. He told me:

> *Always, even as a kid, I could see the thought arising... I wondered why people were so wrapped up in themselves and in thought. I watched other people's lives and they'd appear to be really stuck with their sense of what they are and what they wanted and nothing really mattered to me at all.*

In his early 30s, he had experiences (or perhaps non-experiences is a better word) that confirmed the self was illusion.

> *The realisation came out of the blue that I wasn't doing anything. All the situations that had been in my life were free and there wasn't any attachment to them. There was just this freedom and peace that was unbelievable... Another time I was out at the river fishing with my brother and another bloke... I saw there was nothing there and nothing at all to see. There were just bodies and what the bodies were doing. The third thing—the sense of self appeared to me to be parasitic. There is no past. There is nothing.*

While many mystics search for this insight or awakening and many people meditate for decades to reach such a realisation, Laurie feels it was something that was hard to handle and left him 'between a rock and a hard place'—with a residual body-mind that had to operate in the ordinary world but with an awareness that everyone's perspective, their sense of solid self and their concerns are a self-created illusion.

> *I knew. I had a sense about what was true but I didn't want to go there... It threw up all the fear. I just saw there was nothing. There's no thought about being separate and there's no thought about 'nothing'. There's just nothing there. Anything anyone says about themselves is boasting. Every single thing. We're conditioned. We think there has to be operator for this system to operate but a baby doesn't need a sense of itself to breast feed, giggle and grow up. It's only when they pat me on the head and say 'you're a good boy' or 'bad boy' or whatever that we are conditioned to form a thought 'This is me, this is me, this is me'.*[24]

Barbara Ehrenreich, American author and journalist, describes in *Living with a Wild God* her experience as a young woman and committed atheist. She surmises that sleep deprivation may have been the trigger for this unexpected state of consciousness and, like Laurie, her feelings about the event are much more ambivalent than many commentators.

> *At some moment in my pre-dawn walk... the world flamed into life. How else to describe it... Something poured into me*

> *and I poured out into it. This was not the passive beatific merger with 'the All' as promised by the Eastern mystics. It was a furious encounter with a living substance that was coming at me through all things at once, and one reason for the terrible wordlessness of the experience is that you cannot observe fire without becoming part of it.*[25]

Is she describing the same experience as Irina Tweedie who kept an exceptionally detailed diary of her experiences with a Sufi teacher in India during the 1950s and 1960s?

> *Then it happened. It was as if something snapped inside my head, and the whole of me was streaming out ceaselessly, endlessly, forever, without diminishing, without becoming less... It went on and on. And it was absolute glory. There was no 'me'. Was just flowing. Just being. A feeling of non-ending expansion, just streaming forth. But all this I knew only later, when I tried to analyse it, to remember it... It was shattering. It was wonderful. But what was it? WHAT WAS IT? It could not have been prayer... For a prayer, there must be somebody to pray.*[26]

Another example is quoted in the book *Anaesthesia* by Kate Cole-Adams. She relates the case of a woman having a Caesarean, who woke on the operating table but was paralysed and unable to alert surgeons to her terrible pain. The woman felt she was close to dying but then her consciousness shifted. She said, "It was like I was in the presence of everything that has ever been known by man and everything that ever will be... It was like there was this huge, huge, vast presence and intelligence".[27]

She felt over-awed and also frightened by the immensity.

> *I had this feeling that I had seen something that no human being could ever, in a conscious state be present to and be whole... That it was so vast that the consciousness of human beings—the little consciousness of human beings—unless it was under extraordinary circumstances, shouldn't or couldn't be privy to it.*

In her situation, she felt that she'd been forced there and had to survive it. Like Barbara Ehrenreich, she didn't find it an entirely positive experience.

Perhaps, those without a framework of spiritual understanding or who struggle as the self unexpectedly disappears, fear they will never find their way back to the known.

It hasn't been hard to find many examples of this beyond-self state and I'll explore some others later in the book. What is clear is that, even though all these people report a sense of no solid self, or a self that is dissolved into something greater, there is still something there that is aware and able to relate the experience afterwards.

In short, all these people remained as consciousness even though *self*-consciousness had dissolved.

11

THE HEART OF IT ALL

IN 2011 MY 91-YEAR OLD FATHER was terminally ill with cancer. I flew back to England to spend time with him in his last few months.

There's nothing quite like being close to someone dying to reassess life, death and what we really are. Suddenly the continuity of a person who has been so vital and vibrant is coming to an end. It seems inconceivable that a unique and loved presence will soon be gone and yet we know it happens all the time and will happen to all of us.

My Dad was reviewing his life, telling stories we'd heard before and some we hadn't.

Like many people as they age, he said that inside he didn't feel any different from how he did when he was a 17-year-old. He said he was still exactly the same inside as when he was skating at Pinner ice-rink with his girlfriend, or in his 20s at sea in wartime, or when we were kids paddling in the water at East Wittering.

In one sense that sameness suggests continuity of a person and yet what is it that's the same? Appearance changes, opinions change, mood can change, even our memories shift and remake themselves in new ways, according to scientists.

When we extract all the changeable attributes, what is there but pure consciousness looking through these eyes, hearing through these ears, tasting with this tongue, feeling through this body?

While science can explain many aspects of the self's functioning and brain operation, it cannot yet tell us how consciousness arises.

It doesn't help that there is no agreed definition of exactly what we mean by consciousness. Some people use 'awareness' and 'consciousness' or 'sentience' interchangeably; others make various distinctions.

Consciousness is sometimes equated with the spotlight in the theatre that is turned on particular actors on the stage—this is explored in detail by Bernard J. Baars in *In the Theater of Consciousness.*[28]

He demonstrates how the focus of working consciousness is actually surprisingly limited and can only hold one or two things at a time. Our knowledge and memory are held in the dark archives and items can be retrieved on demand. We have to focus on things in sequence despite some attempts at multi-tasking. The more complex and less habitual the tasks, the harder it is to focus on more than one.

It seems that the brain might have a role in *limiting and focusing* consciousness otherwise there would be an overwhelming input all at once.

And is our consciousness different from an animal's? Some animals, such as elephants, gorillas, dolphins and magpies pass the self-awareness mirror test used on infants.

In this test, the child or animal is marked with a coloured spot while asleep or anesthetised, then placed in front of a mirror. It shows it recognises that the reflection is itself by rubbing or grooming itself to remove the spot.

When scientists explore how physical brain activity aligns with consciousness and perception, they quickly come up against what Australian philosopher David Chalmers calls 'the hard problem' of consciousness. This hard problem is how material activity can give rise to 'qualia'—subjective conscious experiences.

It is easy with our mechanistic 21st century view of the world to almost expect miracles from inanimate objects—computers and smartphones for instance—so we're primed to accept that circuits in the brain might miraculously create a conscious experience with its sight of waving palm trees, taste of a mango, smell of jasmine or sound of flying geese. But science for all its claims and talk of 'artificial intelligence' simply does not know how to bridge the gap between a machine that can 'perceive' to give a programmed response and something that is conscious of its own perception and response.

Admittedly, this ground is relatively new for scientists as consciousness was very much out of fashion for reputable research until this century.

Christof Koch, in collaboration with Francis Crick of DNA fame, is one of vanguards in trying to solve the mystery of consciousness. Koch is looking for the neural correlates of consciousness and has developed an understanding of many aspects of brain activity, as well as developing a framework for further research. He has shown we have neurons that respond only to Jennifer Aniston or Homer Simpson, but does this really get us closer to understanding consciousness?

His work is built on the premise that consciousness and all the qualia somehow arise from neuronal activity. "Consciousness depends on certain coalitions that rest on the properties of very elaborate neural networks."[29]

Bruce Hood, Chair in Developmental Psychology in Society at University of Bristol, in *The Self Illusion,* says, "Every feeling, bit of knowledge and experience you have, or plan to have, is possible because of the cascading activation of neurons. Everything we are, can do and will do is nothing more than this. Otherwise we would need ghosts in the brain and, so far, none have been found".[30]

Similarly, Antonio Damasio, Professor of Neuroscience, Psychology and Neurology, and director of the Brain and Creativity Institute of Southern California, is confident that it is only a matter of time before the mechanics of consciousness are explained. Qualia seem to him to be a more sophisticated neuronal progression of the 'feeling' that causes an amoeba to shrink away from a poke.[31]

I find myself instinctively resistant to this reductionist view.

As I sit at my Dad's side and watch the play of words between us, I know him as something infinitely more than a chatty self-aware computer or a complex amoeba. Whether his responses are mechanical and conditioned from childhood, whether the brain is involved in integrating thought and action, there is a mysterious consciousness looking out of those eyes that, so far, defies all attempts to explain it.

"It's been a wonderful life," he says, though he has had his fair share of challenges.

The most sophisticated robots mimic that consciousness and make us half-believe in their sentience but their eyes are blank and a little scary because something vital is missing. We could program them to comment on their life but we know there is no conscious experience to give it value.

With a little more research, I found that not all scientists believe the mystery of consciousness will be so easily explained.

Neuroscientist Raymond Tallis in *Aping Mankind* takes on the current claims of neuroscience and evolutionary biologists. He highlights both the limitations of the theories and the fundamental problem of how nerve impulses can produce the wonder of consciousness and the myriad experiences of qualia.

He sums it up:

> *So the question still remains: how is it that certain configurations of matter should be aware, should suffer, fear, enjoy and so on? There is nothing in the properties of matter that would lead you to expect that certain configurations of it (human bodies) would pool that experience and live in a public world.* [32]

Although Tallis is no fan of religion or magical thinking he concludes the book with:

> *Criticising the Neuromania and Darwinitis that locates us entirely in the material world is the first step in the task of understanding the place of the human spirit in the great drama of existence and seeing more clearly than we do at present what it is to be a human being. There is no more important or exciting intellectual—or dare I say spiritual—adventure.*

Another neuroscientist, Mario Beauregard, has researched neural activity in Carmelite nuns during mystical experiences. He has identified the ways in which these experiences differ from emotional experiences and is able to systematically address all the materialist arguments that deny the reality of religious or spiritual experience.

In his *The Spiritual Brain,* he states:

> *Consciousness cannot be directly observed. No single brain area is active when we are conscious and idle when we are not. Nor does a specific level of activity in neurons signify that we are conscious. Nor is there a chemistry in neurons that always indicates consciousness.*[33]

His book helps show why "the hard problem of consciousness is simply not resolvable in a materialist frame of reference".

One of the most clearly expressed arguments against the current materialist model of consciousness comes from

British Professor of Philosophy at Rutgers University, Colin McGinn. In *The Mysterious Flame,* he says, "The problem with materialism is that it tries to construct the mind out of properties that refuse to add up to mentality. It assumes that if you put enough pieces of neural chalk together, you will eventually get neural cheese".

He also makes an important stand against the argument that complexity is somehow the secret to generating consciousness:

> *Sheer complexity is irrelevant: merely adding more neurons with more complexity doesn't explain our problem a bit. The problem is how any collection of cells, no matter how large and intricately related, could generate consciousness. The trouble is that neural complexity is the wrong kind of thing to explain consciousness...*

He goes on to point out that if our kidneys had as many cells as our brains, that would not make them conscious.

McGinn takes the 'mysterian' view that consciousness is a mystery that is not solvable within our current frames of reference, and possibly never will be, due to an intrinsic limitation of our perception. He says it is pure dogmatism to assume that things only exist if we can account for them within our current conceptual resources.

> *Indeed, it is nothing short of the idea that the human mind is the measure of reality, a remarkably anthropocentric point of view. We should have the humility, and plain good sense, to admit that*

> *some things may exist without being knowable by us.*

McGinn is not beating a drum for any sort of religious interpretation. His best guess on consciousness is that it may be a quality of space that we are unable to access—except by being conscious.

Dr Robert Lanza, a highly-respected scientist and medical doctor, who has worked in genetics and cell technology, is also prepared to stand against the current tide. In his book *Biocentrism* he says:

> *Consciousness is not just an issue for biologists; it's a problem for physics. Nothing in modern physics explains how a group of molecules in your brain creates consciousness. The beauty of a sunset, the miracle of falling in love, the taste of delicious meal—these are all mysteries to modern science.*[34]

His perspective is that our whole model of the cosmos is faulty because it is missing the role of consciousness. In his words, "There is an underlying problem: we have ignored a critical component of the cosmos, shunted it out of the way because we didn't know what to do with it. This component is consciousness".

He believes few scientists are willing to point out the obvious:

> *During this entire parade, of course, a few people in the crowd will happen to notice that the emperor seems to have skimped in his wardrobe budget. It's one thing to respect authority and*

> *acknowledge that theoretical physicists are brilliant people, even if they do drip food on themselves at buffets. But at some point, virtually everyone has thought or at least felt: This really doesn't work. This doesn't explain anything fundamental, not really. This whole business, A-Z is unsatisfactory. It doesn't ring true. It doesn't feel right. It doesn't answer my questions...*

Roger Penrose, Professor of Mathematics at Oxford University, identifies four possible stances on the question of consciousness, from the most mechanistic view that all thinking is computation and that awareness arises from the complexity of computation, through to the traditional mystical view which says awareness cannot be explained by physical, computational or other scientific terms.[35]

He observes that, if computation added up to consciousness and we could create machines that can duplicate that computation (in addition to being able to undertake complex logical tasks many times faster than we can), they will have immense intelligences of their own and might eventually make us superfluous.

He quotes artificial intelligence philosopher Edward Fredkin who speculates that perhaps, if we are lucky, these new humanoid machines will keep us as pets!

It seems that, although neuroscience can explain many of the responses of this body-mind and the complexity of its reactions, many scientists still believe it's a very long way from explaining consciousness. They are also at a loss to explain how the brain can create a person who experiences or how consciousness could be a by-product of physical processes.

As my dear Dad gets physically weaker, his consciousness of things around him fluctuates but the sense of his presence becomes stronger in the house. He slips into a coma and, after a few days, I know the end is near. It's not the physical symptoms that tell me that but something I can *feel* in the atmosphere.

It feels very similar to the night my daughter was born. Something full and vibrant is in progress. It envelopes my sister and me as we do ordinary things awaiting the inevitable. It connects us to him and to each other. It feels rich and real while also being sad and having a momentous finality.

It's a Friday evening and my sister and I say goodnight to him, even though he is now deeply unconscious. We sleep in the next room with the door open, half listening for him as we doze.

In the early hours of Saturday morning, his breathing stops. His body is cold by daybreak.

We tread quietly and light candles around him. Their light and warmth replace the light and warmth that has disappeared from his still body.

It has been a privilege to witness and be part of this final surrender in all its awful reality.

My watch, which is usually totally reliable, has stopped. Of all the days, of all the hours the battery could reach its end… For me, it's hard not to find meaning in unlikely coincidences.

The sense of Dad's presence seems to be all around my sister and me that morning when we walk on the stony

Pevensey beach nearby, sharing our sadness. It's as if we are seeing part of our own lives disappear, washed away by the tide of years.

Does his consciousness survive somewhere, in some form? Perhaps merged back into the place beyond the self? It's a question that humanity has asked ever since we became self-reflective and aware of death. Perhaps we are framing the question wrongly from our limited viewpoint.

Six years later, when my sister and I go to his grave and plant flowers, I have a strong feeling that he has seen us coming year after year, perhaps perceiving everything at the moment of death, somewhere beyond our worldly perception of time; somewhere that we are never separate.

More recently, I discovered that this perception aligns closely with Indigenous Australians' view of time. What was traditionally translated as 'Dreamtime' might be better translated as 'Everywhen'—probably not a concept most of the early invaders had the inclination to explore.

In the book *Song Spirals* by Gay'Wu Group of Women, the sense of past, present and future overlaid on one another is poetically explained through different glimpses. "Time is co-existing. We are with them. They are in their time. You are in your time. We are in time together. We feel them."[36]

A few years after my Dad's death, my beloved Chandragiri also died. It happened quite unexpectedly.

After slipping and breaking ribs at home, he went to the emergency department at the hospital in York, England, where they discovered advanced liver cancer. He called me in Australia by Skype from his hospital bed and told me that he probably only had a few months to live.

In some ways he sounded almost relieved. I think life had often weighed heavily on him. We talked fondly and he was still joking with the dry humour I'd always loved, despite the shock we were both feeling.

"You are my soul mate," he said.

"You know I've always loved you," I replied.

We agreed to talk again in a few days and, as soon as his face disappeared from the screen, I started thinking about how I could get to England for a while to support him through what I knew would be a difficult time. There was no question that I wanted to be there for him.

The following day I went to move my car back a little in the garage to make space for something and, as I started the engine, the car radio was playing Bob Dylan's *Knocking on Heaven's Door*. Bob Dylan was a favourite of Chandragiri's—he'd been at the infamous concert when Dylan was booed for changing from acoustic to electric guitar—and I immediately knew that death was coming much more quickly than he'd been told. I knew I wouldn't see him again.

I left messages on his mobile but there was no reply.

The following day the news came that he had died.

The day after that, I was admitted to hospital for an emergency gall-bladder operation, grieving even though I felt close to him and our final conversation had been a blessing and a fitting goodbye.

With various drips, drugs, anaesthetics and procedures, I passed the next few days in a strange and uncomfortable alien world.

Jamie was visiting me with concern—as always, a lifeline when I needed it—and a blessing of love in a sterile hospital environment. But how can you fully share with one man that you're grieving for another? Somehow our models of relationships don't allow the complexity of feelings, that love can flow in more than one direction.

I was home in time to keep vigil through the night while Chandragiri's cremation service was held on the other side of the world. He felt close and still does sometimes.

I certainly don't have the answer to what lies beyond death. I feel our understanding is so primitive we cannot hope to know from our limited perspective in time and space. We do not even fully understand the consciousness of living.

But I do know, as surely as I can know anything, that love is never lost. I sense it lives beyond time and is bigger than our personal tamed versions. Sometimes we are lucky enough to walk a little while with people who help us tune into its power and who melt our separate self into the unity of all that is.

12

WHAT ABOUT GOD?

MY EXPERIENCE AND MY RESEARCH had shown me beyond reasonable doubt that there are times we human beings can transcend our usual self-anchored perspective and experience something so real, so awe-inspiring, so blissful that it transforms lives.

It also became clearer and clearer that this sort of transcendental consciousness aligns very well with enduring ideas of God and heaven.

From my childhood catechism to the writing of prophets, mystics and sages across the centuries, I find God described in surprisingly consistent ways.

If I reject the descriptions of a super-human father in heaven, which are so often taken literally and overlaid with the child-like framework of rules, reward and punishment, there is still something that needn't be in conflict with current science or our more sophisticated times.

Of course, one of the first things the mystics tell is us

that God is beyond mental knowing or definition.

In the Hindu tradition the ultimate Brahman is not an object and is beyond the reach of the senses or mind. *'Neti neti'*, Sanskit for 'Not this, not this' is often used in relation to Brahman to discard definitions. This is similar to the Muslim insistence that Allah is indefinable and cannot be depicted.

Famous 13th century Christian mystic Meister Eckhart said, "Do not imagine that your reason can grow to the knowledge of God".[37]

St Hesychios the Priest taught, "The blessed divine light will illuminate the heart to the degree that pure Consciousness is purged of all concepts and ideas".[38]

The Sufis, the mystical practitioners of Islam, have no argument with that. A traditional Sufi saying proclaims, "Someone who looks for God through logical proof is like someone who looks for the sun with a lamp".

Abd Al-Kader says, "Whatever you think concerning Allah—know that he is different from that!"[39]

Nisagaddata Maharaj, 20th century mystic, said, "The mind shapes the language and the language shapes the mind... Words can bring you only up to their own limit; to go beyond, you must abandon them. Remain as the silent witness only".

In the *Bhagavad Gita*, the ancient Indian text written before Christ, Krishna tells Arjuna:

> *When thy mind leaves behind its dark forest of delusion, thou shalt go beyond the scriptures of times past and still to come.*

When thy mind, which may be wavering in the contradictions of many scriptures, shall rest unshaken in divine contemplation, then the goal of Yoga is thine.[40]

When something is so far beyond everyday experience, it's not surprising that reports differ in their emphasis.

Like the proverbial blind men who feel different parts of an elephant, everyone comes back with a different part of the picture. "It's like a rope," says the one who feels the tail. "It's like a tree-trunk," says the one who feels the leg. "It's like a spear," says the one who feels the tusk. All those people who have had a deeper revelation are trying to convey something beyond their normal senses.

Despite a few differences in emphasis, I found that reports across the ages have much in common when describing the experience of God or expanded consciousness.

There are ten attributes that seem to be common in different eras and cultures:

Beyond description
Infinite/beyond time
Beyond place/everywhere
All knowing (omniscient)
All powerful (omnipotent)
Awe-inspiring
Consciousness/beingness
Blissful/joyful
Love
Inseparable unity, oneness.

The descriptions of an experience beyond self in Chapter 10 include many of these adjectives or convey a similar meaning.

Here are a few more beyond-self experiences that show striking similarities to ancient descriptions of God.

Andrew Cohen, a contemporary teacher born in 1955, relates his spontaneous realisation at age 16 while visiting Rome. He had been sitting talking to his mother and there was no obvious reason for what happened next:

> *It's hard to really explain rationally but the experience was that I suddenly became aware of the whole universe... It became apparent to me that the entire universe, the entire cosmic process was self-aware... And the ultimate nature of the whole process, which I was an inseparable part of, was a kind of an impersonal absolute love that was physically overwhelming and almost physically excruciating to experience... I became aware in that moment that there was no such thing as death. And that all points in space were exactly the same place.*

Mario Beauregard, the neuroscientist mentioned earlier, in his book *The Spiritual Brain,* relates his own all-encompassing realisation in terms that are classically similar to those used by mystics from every tradition.

> *Suddenly I merged with the infinitely loving Cosmic Intelligence (or Ultimate Reality) and became united with everything in the cosmos. The unitary state of being, which transcends the subject/object duality, was timeless and accompanied by intense bliss and ecstasy...*[41]

John Maynard, the friend I first met at college and who has subsequently spent much of his life in Indian ashrams, describes his first taste of a shift in perspective.

> *I was around 17 or 18 and I had hitched down to Brockwood Park in Hampshire—the Krishnamurti school, where he was holding a series of public talks. I was dropped off at the bottom of the drive late in the evening and the whole place was bathed in moonlight... As it was one of those rare warm English summer nights, I spread out my sleeping-bag on the ground and went to sleep. About 2am or 3am, my body woke up but there was no 'I', no I-centre at all. Instead there was complete knowledge of everything. The universe was all one thing. One knowledge. Reflecting on it later, I knew that if I had asked any question, the answer would have instantly been there. The whole thing lasted just a few minutes...*[42]

John Thornton, Associate Professor at the School of Information and Communication Technology at Griffith University relates a similar experience of 'all knowingness' at age 18 or 19. His shift was brought on by psilocybin mushrooms:

> *I fell into an altered state. The knowledge came to me that this was the state Jesus was in—that was the only thing in the culture I knew at the time that I could relate it to—it wasn't 'I am Jesus' or anything but 'Jesus was in a state like this. That is why he was saying what he was saying. I understand now.' It was an experience of what seemed to be total knowledge. I*

> *knew whatever I looked at I could see right into it. You could ask me anything and I would know. I knew whatever I looked at couldn't help but open itself up to me—I had this penetrating consciousness.*

When I asked him if this could have been a drug-induced delusion of some sort, he replied:

> *I don't feel it was a delusion… There was a higher degree of reality than the reality I was living then, or that I am living in now. I wasn't hallucinating. It was obvious to me that humanity is living in a narrowed-down, unperceptive thought world. There was a sense 'This is home. This is where I belong. This is where everyone belongs' and that the state of ordinary life is a degradation of what we really are.*[43]

An interesting aside here is that *New Scientist* reported a study in 2006 that gave volunteers either psilocybin or an active placebo, Ritalin. More than one-third of the volunteers on psilocybin reported a 'complete mystical experience' and that it was the most spiritually significant experience of their lifetimes. No-one who took Ritalin said the same.[44]

The report says the precise action of psilocybin on brain function remains elusive.

While some scientists will be keen to conclude that such evidence shows spiritual experience is only a chemical brain delusion, can we ignore the certainty people have that their perception was more real than everyday experience?

Is it not possible that the neurochemical actually deactivates a brain function that normally interferes with or creates a barrier to perceiving a greater reality?

(It's worth noting that psilocybin and similar drugs can also have much less pleasant effects such as severe paranoia and anxiety, and can be dangerous under uncontrolled circumstances—so don't try this at home, children!)

I found a fascinating book *Dancing with the Void* about a farmer's son, Emmanuel Sorensen, born in Denmark in 1890, who seemed to have retained a thin self-concept from a young age. He also equated that with a knowledge of God.

> *From infancy, I was ego-free, desire-free, plan-free and carefree... Neither mind nor ego was developed to be any trouble during seven or even the first fourteen years of my solitary childhood... The mystic Silence ... was the silence of desire and thought. In the freedom of solitude, God was clearly immanent. God simply was... unhidden by ideas, unblurred by words. I did not think of or to God. All was real and simple.*[45]
>
> (His original text never used the words 'I' or 'me' but editors felt adding them made his meaning clearer.)

Many years later, Emmanuel met Ramana Maharshi who called him 'a natural born mystic' and gave him the name Sunyata. This unusual, humble man lived most of his life in India with no money and few possessions yet some of the 20th century's most influential thinkers counted him amongst their friends. He was close to poet Rabindranath

Tagore, was often a guest of the Nehru family, lived on author Alan Watts' houseboat and had a lifelong friendship with Lama Govinda.

In the book, Sunyata also quotes poet Alfred Tennyson's experience of the no-self state:

> *A kind of waking trance I have frequently had quite from boyhood, when I have been alone... All at once, as it were... the individuality itself seemed to dissolve and fade away into boundless Being. This was not a confused state, but the clearest of the clearest, the surest of the surest, the weirdest of the weirdest, utterly beyond words, where death was an almost laughable impossibility, the loss of personality was the only true Life.*

Krishnamurti relates the story of a businessman who came to him desperate to regain an experience he had had a couple of years before. This is part of the man's description:

> *From the moment I came out of my front door I had a strange feeling of lightness, as though I was walking on air... Every little object, which ordinarily I would never have noticed, seemed to have an extraordinary quality of its own and, strangely, everything seemed to be a part of me. Nothing was separate from me; in fact, the 'me' as the observer, the perceiver, was absent... Everything was alive and I loved everything. I was the scent of the flowers, but there was no 'me' to smell the flowers... There was no separation between me and them... Time had stopped; there was no past, present or future...*[46]

He goes on to say that all the goodness and compassion of the world was in that park, and 'God' was there. Although he had no religious belief and little time for churches, he sensed a Being in whom all things lived and had their being.

These reports, and many more, give a surprisingly consistent view of this 'beyond self' state and many people spontaneously name it God.

While these descriptions fit closely with descriptions of God from religious texts, can I conclude that this formless God is also our creator? I know one of biggest areas of argument between scientists and religious pundits is the role of God as creator of the world and that needs more exploration.

13

A CREATOR GOD?

I WONDER HOW MANY TIMES I recited as a child, "I believe in God the Father Almighty, creator of heaven and earth".

The story of God creating the world in six days and resting on the seventh was there from my early childhood and I can remember trying to memorise which bits he added on which days.

I can even vaguely remember drawing the output of each day in coloured pencils on very poor paper, which didn't easily absorb the colour and tore if I pressed too hard. The fifth and sixth days, which brought forth the fish and birds and then the animals, were my favourites, inspiring clumsy attempts to draw elephants, giraffes, camels and lions.

Since Darwin, that notion of creation, taken literally, has been a very easy one for science to demolish. And, as scientists swept that story off the table, they felt they had consigned any notion of God to the garbage. But not so fast.

What if our indefinable God, which is more of a conscious, intelligence innate in the universe than a man in sandals, is integral to everything that unfolds? That it has been integral since the beginning and even before our notion of the beginning at the Big Bang?

Then Darwinism is quite compatible with God and evolution is a manifestation of God in action.

If a creative Source capable of setting this whole universe in motion exists, it would be fair to assume it is so far beyond our three-dimensional understanding that it would only be intuited in its manifestations.

It would also be reasonable to think that any people who had glimpsed this reality through the ages would have tried to capture it in images and symbols that are constrained by the extent of their knowledge, the limits of language and the known world to compare it to.

The idea of creator God transcends different cultures but most speak of a single being who was responsible.

A few years ago, in a book I picked up at a market stall, I found a lovely Creation Hymn from the *Rig Veda* (one of the oldest known texts in an Indo-European language, thought to have been written around 1700-2300 BC). It intuits the time before time and the emergence of a universe. It begins…

Then even nothingness was not, nor existence.
There was no air then, nor the heavens beyond it.
What covered it? Where was it? In whose keeping?
Was there then cosmic water in depths unfathomed?

Then there were neither death nor immortality,
Nor was there then the torch of night and day.
The One breathed windlessly and self-sustaining.
There was that One then, and there was no other.

At first there was only darkness wrapped in darkness.
All this was only unillumined water.
That One which came to be, enclosed in nothing,
Arose at last, born of the power of heat.[47]

This ancient understanding is also reflected in the Hindu *Maitri Upanishad,* which says, "In the beginning all was Brahman, one and infinite. He is beyond north and south, and east and west, and beyond what is above or below. His infinity is everywhere".

It goes on to say, "He alone is awake in eternity. Then from his infinite space new worlds arise and awake, a universe which is a vastness of thought. In the consciousness of Brahman, the universe is, and into him it returns".[48]

The *Svetasvatara Upanishad* speaks of Brahman as "The God whose light illumines all creation, the Creator of all from the beginning. He was, he is and forever he shall be. He is in all and he sees all".

In India, this story of the emergence of the universe is acknowledged every month. The night of darkness before the new moon is known as Shivaratri and commemorates the darkness of the uncreated cosmos before Shiva brought the universe and time into being. The most significant Shivaratri each year—Mahashivaratri—falls in February or March and is a major festival when people fast all night and then celebrate Shiva's dance of creation with the new moon.

The Native Americans also believe in a 'Great Spirit' who predated many other godlike figures and had a role in creating them.

An Ancient Egyptian text says, "The Lord of All, after having come into being says, I am he who came into being as Khepri (the Becoming One). When I came into being, all the beings came into being after I became".[49]

The Mesoamerican cosmogony begins with Ometecuhtli, who is self-created 'Lord of Duality' and appeared in male and female aspects as Ometeotl and Omecihuatl.

In some traditions, God is female but still has the same power of creation and sustains the universe.

As Diana Eck, Professor of Comparative Religion and Indian Studies at Harvard University, explains the Indian philosophy developed through the *Devi Mahatmya* and *Devi Bhagavata Purana* texts, "The Goddess is the All—indescribable and ultimately ungraspable... She is the Supreme Being, the ground of all Reality".[50]

The Hindu *Devi Mahatmya* says, "By you is everything supported, by you is the world created, by you it is protected, O Goddess, and you always consume it at the end (of time)".[51]

Although we can classify the various stories of creation as myths, we do the term 'myth' a disservice if we simply use it as synonym for 'untruth' or 'legend'. Myths, as Jung and Joseph Campbell powerfully demonstrated, are the symbols with which we can understand deeper truths. Science, in trying to destroy myths, is not only destroying superstitious stories but taking away a symbolic representation of meaning.

In *The Hero with a Thousand Faces,* Joseph Campbell says of the mythological stories, "It will always be the one, shape-shifting yet marvellously constant story that we find, together with a challengingly persistent suggestion of more remaining to be experienced than will ever be known or told".[52]

Perhaps if we stop taking these myths out of context and seeing them as fanciful stories for primitive people, we can discover a wealth of reflections on humanity's search for meaning. We will also discover a widespread intuition of a numinous creativity or intelligence involved in creating the universe.

There are so many factors in the universe that are so finely tuned to support the possibility of life that even scientists concede that the probability of them occurring by chance are infinitesimally tiny.

In particular the amount of dark matter and temperature variations in the background radiation are crucial to constraining the acceleration with which the universe is expanding, and to allowing matter to clump together to form solid solar systems.

As Robert Lanza expresses it in *Biocentrism*:

> *By the late sixties it had become clear that if the Big Bang had been just one part in a million more powerful, the cosmos would have blown outward too fast to allow stars and worlds to form... Even more coincidentally, the universe's four forces*

> *and all of its constants are just perfectly set up for atomic interactions, the existence of atoms and elements, planets, liquid water and life. Tweak any of them and you never existed.*[53]

He goes on to provide a two-page table of all the finely-tuned, life-friendly essential constants.

The scale and complexity of where we live is increasingly awe-inspiring the more deeply we look into it. Science hasn't so much explained everything away as uncovered a whole new layer of questions.

Mathematical physicists like Brian Greene have come up with incredible theories to explain this fine-tuning—not least an infinite number of universes with every variation of physical laws so one ends up having the right variation to support life![54]

In fact, there are many variations on the parallel universe theory, from a 'quilted multiverse' to a simulated multiverse—living inside a computer simulation.

At even more microscopic levels, string theory has generated much interest as potentially being the missing link in the theory of everything—more specifically, it seeks to unite quantum mechanics and general relativity, particle theories and gravity.

A string, if it exists, is rather like an infinitesimally small string floating in space-time. Like the string of a musical instrument, it is under tension and when 'plucked' gives off elementary particles rather than notes. A string is thought to be about 10^{-33} centimetres (a millionth of a billionth of a billionth of a billionth of a centimetre).

There are string theories with open strings and closed loops, and particles called fermions and bosons—and, because the strings are too small to be visible to any instruments, only incredibly complex mathematical equations can prove or disprove a string model.

Apparently, there are 10^{500} possible string theories, which one of the fathers of string theory, Professor Leonard Susskind, welcomes as this gives the probability that some strings will generate life-friendly universes!

Could God be pulling the strings?!

Dark energy is another mystery—or what Smithsonian magazine in a 2010 article called 'The biggest mystery of the universe'. The article explains,

> *Astronomers have compiled evidence that what we've always thought of as the actual universe—me, you, this magazine, planets, stars, galaxies, all the matter in space—represents a mere 4 percent of what's actually out there. The rest they call, for want of a better word, dark: 23 percent is something they call dark matter, and 73 percent is something even more mysterious, which they call dark energy.*

The article goes on to say that, in 2003, the National Research Council called the nature of dark energy one of the most pressing scientific problems of the coming decades and that cosmologist Michael S. Turner of University of Chicago ranks dark energy as 'the most profound mystery in all of science'. The article concludes with an acknowledgement that there is still much that is unknown.

Scientific American confirms, "It is not really known whether or not the universe started from a singularity. Our measurements can take us back only so far; ideas about the nature of the cosmos at the start of the big bang are mostly unproved conjecture".[55]

Whichever way we try to grasp this, we come up against the limits of the mind to conceive of how something could have appeared from nothing—infinite different universes are probably even more inconceivable than a handful of similar universes—or how anything could have always existed—be that God or the potential for all this matter to have existed within 'nothing' or a tiny seed.

As beings in time who know only things with a beginning and end, our minds are powerless to go beyond the idea of the Big Bang or to explain how or where the potential existed before that defining moment of our current scientific understanding.

Surely at this point, as science uncovers ever more wonders and complex questions, we have to say 'We don't know'—that an innate intelligence within and beyond things is at least as likely as infinite chaos that eventually produced order.

Or, as British astrophysicist Arthur Eddington said about the uncertainty principle in physics, "Something unknown is doing we don't know what".

I think it is quite valid to conceive of the possibility of something beyond our materialistic boundaries as the source or ground of life—a more sophisticated update of the intuition that gave us the myth of the hands-on, father-like creator? I'm not suggesting any humanoid look-alike with a

DIY kit here but something that is in the essence of life and, as the Muslims contend, beyond form or description.

Before we leave the topic of creation, for me, one of the most potent symbols of a creative God is the Shiva Nataraja (dancing Shiva).

In 2007, I went to Chidambaram in South India to the temple where the familiar brass statue of Shiva Nataraja had its origin. It's an incredible place of pillared halls, *brahmin* priests in white robes with their sacred thread across one bare shoulder, and huge decorative gateways to the four cardinal directions.

I felt I had stepped back a few thousand years to a time and place when ritual still had immense power and the divine loomed large in daily life. The clanging of bells, the incense, the visual feast of fire offering and the seclusion from the outside world are perhaps designed to fill the senses and still the mind.

At the appointed hour, a golden statue is brought out by a *brahmin* from its hidden shrine and held aloft amidst a cacophony of noise. The crowd all strains towards it. Then it is gone again behind the curtain—perhaps like all our glimpses of the divine from this human place.

I find the symbol of dancing Shiva is a particularly relevant one because it is not about a one-off creative event that happened in the distant mists of pre-history but a God that is continuing to dance the universe into being. The dancing god in a circle of flames has many layers of symbolic meaning.

Traditionally, after his manifestation as motionless Shiva, deep in silent meditation, Shiva Nataraja rises and "the countless trillions upon zillions of rhythms and pulses of Creation start their beat, for all of Nature is dance: the dance of wind and waves, the rounds of seasons and tides, the swirls of planets and galaxies…".[56]

Shiva, in the Hindu tradition, is both creator and destroyer—a symbol that embraces the interconnected cyclical nature of reality.

In 2004, the Indian government donated a two-metre tall statue of Shiva Nataraja to CERN, the European Center for Research in Particle Physics in Geneva. It celebrates the research centre's long association with India and acknowledges the metaphor of Shiva's dance for the cosmic dance of subatomic particles, which is observed and analysed by CERN's physicists.

Author Fritjof Capra's international bestseller *The Tao of Physics,* first published in 1975, also used Shiva Nataraja as a central metaphor in exploring physicists' contemporary understanding. He said:

> *Hundreds of years ago, Indian artists created visual images of dancing Shivas in a beautiful series of bronzes. In our time, physicists have used the most advanced technology to portray the patterns of the cosmic dance. The metaphor of the cosmic dance thus unifies ancient mythology, religious art and modern physics.*[57]

It has become increasingly clear to me that, whatever God is, it is not a distant creator but something that is a power both beyond and within creation, something way outside our three-dimensional perception but occasionally glimpsed when noisy world concerns and self-consideration are silenced.

I'm not sure it's the sort of something that wants to be worshipped or prayed to but it's the sort of something that generates awe. It is love as well as consciousness. It's something the individual self can dissolve into—or realise it has always been a part of.

It also seems to be an integral part of the dance of creation. As Krishna says in the *Bhagavad Gita,* "He is invisible: He cannot be seen. He is far and he is near. He moves and he moves not. He is within all and he is outside all".[58]

A.H. Almaas—who worked on his Physics Ph. D. at University of California in Berkeley before turning to spiritual and psychological aspects of life—devotes his whole book *Luminous Night's Journey* to painstakingly describing the process of his deepening consciousness. He recounts the realisation of what he calls the 'universal witness'. Like many of the other descriptions of beyond-self, it sounds very much like our ideas of God.

> *I am a silent witness, vast and unchanging, beyond time and all space... I am unchanging. I am deathless. I am unborn. I am uncaused, unoriginated. I was never born, will never die... I am beyond space and time; both space and time are within me... Mind is within me, small and always trying to grasp me.*[59]

14

MASTERS OF NON-DUALITY

IT WAS READING MORE about consciousness and how that related to brain, self and perhaps something beyond, that introduced me to the 'non-duality' concept.

In 2003 I picked up a book called *Consciousness Speaks* by Ramesh Balsekar.

Ramesh was a graduate of the University of London and a General Manager of the Bank of India before his retirement in 1977, giving him perfect communication skills to translate Indian traditions into English. He had been a disciple of Nisagadatta Maharaj, a highly regarded sage of the twentieth century, and translated discourses for him before achieving his own realisation in 1982. Ramesh is one of a continuing tradition of Indian masters in the *Advaita Vedanta* (non-duality) tradition.

In 2007, I visited Ramesh in his apartment in Mumbai where 20-30 people gathered each morning for his teaching. We all waited outside an older residential building in the upmarket suburb of Breach Candy, before being summoned upstairs for a relaxed talk in an unpretentious living room.

He seemed to me to be a very simple and humble man with keen intelligence and perception. His books cover quite a range of styles from logical philosophical discourse to more practical applications of the non-dual perspective.

Almost until his death, he was following the daily routine of welcoming people to his unspectacular apartment and answering their questions with down-to-earth honesty and clarity. There was no big-guru fanfare or following and he definitely didn't encourage the disciple mentality or people worshipping him as a master. He used to say 'No-one is invited, and everyone is welcome'.

Ramesh's discourses and books helped me to join up the dots of the different bits of knowledge and insights into a more coherent philosophy. He particularly helped clarify for me how this Julia body-mind should live after the knowledge that her 'self' is a conceptual overlay. But before I talk more about that, a little more about *Advaita Vedanta* …

Fast forward to another trip to India and I'm tracking down the 'father of *Advaita*'.

Within jet-engine roar of Kochi airport in Kerala, beside a typical Indian road that is a turbulent river of brightly painted trucks, overloaded buses, beetling scooters carrying multiple family members, honking black and yellow auto-rickshaws and an increasing number of cars vying for spaces, there is a strange hexagonal, maroon-painted tower.

It sits in what appears to be a school car-park on the opposite side of the road to tea-stalls with plastic chairs, fruit-stalls and a tangle of human traffic finding its way purposefully along a dusty, rubble-paved roadside strip.

It wasn't quite what I expected for the village where Shankara, one of India's most influential philosophers, was born. I'd imagined a quiet temple beside the river, perhaps a few Indian pilgrims, probably a souvenir shop but space to sit and contemplate the meaning of life.

My Christian taxi driver, with a rosary hanging over his rear-view mirror, where in other parts of India there is more likely to be a Ganesh or *rudraksha* beads, felt it his duty to accompany me inside.

The other visitors were a large party of young men and older women dressed totally in black. They were fasting as part of their Sabarimala pilgrimage, which does not allow participation by women of menstruating age.

The young men were wild-eyed, musky smelling and full of the hyper-energy that comes at a certain stage of fasting. They rushed in groups of three or four around the spiral walkways that led higher into the tower, stopping beside the various tableaux and statues for a moment's seemingly genuine reverence before dashing on to the next level.

The tableaux were fairly crudely sculpted and garishly painted scenes that said nothing of Shankara's philosophy, only the miraculous stories that helped ensure his name was passed down through many generations and cemented in folk memory.

According to a postcard bought at the ticket kiosk, Shankara was born in 509 BC but this supposed date may have more to do with the little town of Kalady wanting to trumpet a special festival celebrating 1500 years since the auspicious birth—as tattered and faded posters from 2009 declared.

While scholars agree on Shankara's likely existence as a real historical figure, his dates are the subject of speculation and debate. Different experts put his birth anywhere between 44 BC and 805 CE. The legend states a short life of 32 or 33 years.

After being childless and praying to Shiva, his mother is said to have had to choose between a short-lived genius or a long-lived dullard. She chose the former—but one academic argued he must have lived to more than 90 years of age to complete all the works attributed to him.

But I wasn't so much concerned with the colourful myths or historical research. I was interested in the philosophy attributed to him and his role in drawing together earlier Indian traditions with mystical experience and logical debate to leave a lasting legacy to India's spiritual perspective.

The legends have him debating with the greatest thinkers and spiritual authorities of his day and winning through with both logic and the authority of his own deeper experience. As a charismatic teacher and inspirational exponent of a new way of thought, he has the influential status of a Plato or Buddha or Jesus or Mohammad, though much less well known in the west.

His thinking underpins the Indian school of *Advaita Vedanta* and the way truth is expressed by many later Indian gurus and saints right up to the present day. Although he is often thought of as originator the tradition, there is evidence that the roots of the *Advaita* philosophy pre-date him by hundreds or even thousands of years.

Advaita or non-duality is the perception that reality is all one thing, that 'oneness' is the underlying truth and all the diversity is a more superficial layer of play.

The essence of the philosophy is that Brahman (the Absolute) alone is real; that this world has only relative reality and that the *atman* (the individual soul) is not different from Brahman. In fact, nothing is different from Brahman because that would be duality. Shankara said:

> *Talk as much philosophy as you like, worship as many gods as you please, observe ceremonies and sing devotional hymns, but liberation will never come, even after a hundred aeons, without realising the Oneness.*[60]

Living in a world where our focus is very much on discreet, solid objects and on the mental activities of defining, separating and discriminating, I understand this can seem a very dubious and intangible claim to anyone coming across it for the first time but, for me, it was the missing link.

It is a concept that makes perfect sense and aligns with a wide range of mystical and religious experience, as well as being compatible with emerging scientific revelations.

At the most material level, science tells us that nothing new is added to the original matter of the universe—it was all one before the Big Bang and "the cosmos was a singular and perfectly symmetric unity".[61]

Every atom of our bodies and of our world is part of an

unbroken unfolding and an exchange of elements. As Dr Darryl Reanney, an Australian microbiologist, put it:

> *Our bodies are made of star ash. We are children of the stars... We do not merely sample the universe we live in, rather we are seamlessly part of that universe. We are the gift of many stars, the flesh of many creatures, the waters of many rivers... We are still all we once were.*[62]

Although it is not something we can experience, we believe science when it tells us that we are much more space than solid.

If we could see at an atomic level, our bodies and brains would be 99 percent empty space. Some commentators say the whole human race could be condensed into the size of a sugar cube, or the universe into a baseball, if all the space within the atoms could be removed.

If we could see at that level, the boundaries of our body would also be invisible, with a constant exchange of molecules to and from the environment. Boundaries are a result of our relative size and the focus of our viewing.

Even before we die, an atom that was in our skin last month may be part of the earth today and in a water-plant next week. Next month, it may part of a fish and, next year, part of our friend's heart.

Advaita Vedanta is not simply saying that all we are is particles of matter though—there is more to it than that. Brahman is the formless consciousness and this is the singularity of the universe.

This makes the whole cosmic creation not the work of a distant creator God but an intrinsic intelligence that is both the whole thing and present in every tiny part. Creation was not a distant event but is a constant becoming.

As Christian mystic Meister Eckhart also said, "God is creating the whole universe, full and entire, in this present moment".[63]

Or as A.H. Almaas says, "The whole universe is like a fountain, always unfolding, always pouring out in different forms—but always remaining water, that is Being or presence".

Advaita says the ultimate Brahman is infinite, changeless, self-existent and it is also described by the Sanskrit term *satchitananda* which is translated as 'being-consciousness-bliss'. *Satchitananda* is not only an attribute but is also the *essence* of the ultimate reality.

Shankara said, "Now finally and clearly I know that I am the *atman* whose nature is eternal joy. I see nothing, I hear nothing. I know nothing that is separate from me".[64]

If God is consciousness and God is non-dual, it follows that everything is consciousness.

One of *Adviata's* most respected texts, the *Ashtavakra Gita* says, "It is you that pervades this universe, and the universe exists in you. Your true nature is pure consciousness".[65]

This belief is close to what is known as 'panpsychism'—the belief that the soul or mind is in everything. Variations of this perspective are not only found in the ancient Indian texts but also amongst the ancient Greek philosophers, Taoism and later philosophers, such as Schopenhauer and William James.

A similar belief 'pantheism'—God in everything—also has a long history.

Spinoza, 17th century philosopher, is thought of as the godfather of pantheism, although its origins are much older. Spinoza argued with Descartes' mind-body dualism, denied a personal god and was considered one of the great rationalists. But he did believe in God.

He said, "Whatsoever is, is in God, and without God nothing can be, or be conceived". He clearly explained his concept of God, "My opinion concerning God differs widely from that which is ordinarily defended by modern Christians. For I hold that God is of all things the cause immanent, as the phrase is, not transient".[66]

Strangely Spinoza's view that there is nothing that is not God has led to him being called an atheist whereas, in fact, he was described by the poet Novalis as "a man who was drunk with God", a term that is often used of mystics like the Sufis who see God everywhere and in everything.

Einstein, also acknowledged a God that is somehow intrinsic to the laws of nature, "I believe in Spinoza's God, who reveals Himself in the lawful harmony of the world, not in a God who concerns Himself with the fate and the doings of mankind".

The God that is the living reality of everything has also been expressed by poets. In the poem *Tintern Abbey,* Wordsworth speaks of a joyful presence he felt, "whose dwelling is the light of setting suns, And the round ocean and living air, And the blue sky, and in the mind of man: A motion and spirit that impels all thinking things, all objects of all thought, And rolls through all things".

Contemporary philosopher David Chalmers in *The Character of Consciousness* has proposed a variation of this as the 'missing link' between matter and consciousness. He says, "We have good reason to suppose that consciousness has a fundamental place in nature" and that "consciousness and physical reality are deeply intertwined".[67]

Stuart Kauffman, biologist and emeritus professor of biochemistry at the University of Pennsylvania, has speculated on the precursors to consciousness being in the smallest living things. In speaking of a bacterium swimming up a glucose gradient, he explains that the bacterium not only requires a receptor for glucose but must also have a means of interpreting the sign and 'knowing' that glucose is good. Kauffman says:

> *Without attributing consciousness to the bacterium, we can see in this capacity the evolutionary onset of choice and thus of meaning, value, doing and purpose... Neither signs, interpretations nor mistakes are possible in physics where only happenings occur. Thus, meaning has entered the universe: the local glucose gradient is a sign that means glucose is—probably—nearby.*[68]

Complexity theory biologists, like Stuart Kauffmann and Harold Morowitz are therefore saying that matter is intrinsically aware—right down to the level of electrons, which maintain separation and structure.

Quantum physicist David Bohm, once tagged 'the next

Einstein', also noted that the apparently chaotic movements of electrons managed to produce highly ordered arrangements. These trillions of particles all behaved as if they knew what the others were doing. He commented, "Such quantum wholeness of activity is closer to the organised unity of functioning of the parts of a living being than it is to the kind of unity that is obtained by putting together the parts of a machine".[69]

While these perspectives are still very much analysing from the material viewpoint, they are compatible with the perspective of *Advaita.*

Before we leave Shankara, it's worth noting that, although he taught non-duality, he also saw a role for different levels of religion or spiritual experience.

For those who could not grasp the profound but impersonal concept of non-duality, he acknowledged the role gods and goddesses play in bringing the individual closer to an understanding and experience of their true reality. His own expression of realisation mixes both the duality of a supplicant with a broader perspective:

Oh Lord! Pardon my three sins.
I have in contemplation clothed thee in form—Thee who art formless.
I have in praise described Thee who art ineffable.
And in visiting temples ignored Thy omnipresence.

In India, what may be seen superficially as a crazy pagan pantheon is actually a vibrant smorgasbord of different aspects of God. There is room for devotion to the individual god or goddess that resonates for the individual but also a widespread acknowledgement that they are perspectives of the one formless, indefinable God.

Confusingly for the outsider, someone who is referring to an ultimate reality may also refer to it as Brahma, Shiva, Vishnu, Krishna, Durga, Kali or Devi (the goddess) if they are seeing beyond the simple symbolism of their preferred manifestation.

Parvati, the goddess bride of Shiva in Hindu myth, in her description of him, repeats a theme that is familiar from so many religions, "He is unchanging, indescribable, eternal, though he assumes shapes and forms for the welfare of his devotees".

Importantly, in acknowledging an all-encompassing spirit beyond the myriad images of god, Hindu tradition agrees with Christianity, Judaism and Islam that there is only one God.

Where *Advaita Vedanta* differs from everyday interpretation of all these religions though is in its totally non-dual approach. Not only is there only one God. There is only one. Full stop.

Good and evil, heaven and hell, birth and death, people and planets have only relative reality as part of the one unchanging, absolute reality. Gold may be shaped into the form of a serpent or a saint but it is still gold.

On a few occasions, I have visited Arunachala Mountain in Tamil Nadu, where my old college friend John lives within sight of the mountain.

Arunachala is revered as a sacred mountain, said by some to be one of the oldest mountains on earth and associated with the myth of Shiva as an infinite pillar of flame. It was also the home of sage Ramana Maharshi who attracted people from around the world in the first half of the twentieth century. Today, many pilgrims still come to his ashram, climb the rocky mountain paths or walk the 14 kilometres around the mountain's base.

On one of my visits, I scrambled up the mountain path in the heat to reach the cave where Ramana Maharshi spent many years before his ashram was established. This elevated spot looks down over the ancient temple with its highly decorated towers in the town of Tiruvannamalai and has panoramic views across the sun-baked plains.

The noise from traffic, auto-rickshaws and the general Indian cacophony were a distant hum carried on the breeze from below. I stood and breathed the warm morning air, letting my eyes rest on the distant scene while minutes passed. My mind stilled and there was peace. A thought of Ramana arose and, within the stillness of my mind, I heard the words, "I see through your eyes. You see through mine".

15

THE PAIN AND PURPOSE OF SEPARATION

IT SEEMS TO ME THAT one of the underlying themes of my life has been separation.

One of my very earliest memories—at barely three years old—was being left with another little girl to play, while my mother disappeared down the street with my new baby sister in the pram. I yelled in anguish for however long it took her to complete the shopping and return for me! Then there were the playtimes alone at school when I was kept inside for not eating lunch. And later the lingering sense that I didn't quite fit with the rest of society and its preoccupations.

Often relationships that had been a doorway to love and a sense of connection ended in separation, sometimes by my own hand. Deciding on a life in Australia, away from most of my family and loved ones in England, was another decision for separation, even though I didn't see it through that lens at the time.

I remember a particular occasion, not long after we had moved to Brisbane, sitting in a café in the city on a beautifully bright, winter morning and feeling an existential anguish of separation. I knew that wherever I was, I was always separate from something or someone I loved.

I couldn't be simultaneously in Australia and England and India and Greece; I couldn't be with each of the people I loved—every choice was a loss of something of essential value. Some separations, such as those through the end of relationships or death, were irreversible and the feeling of loss in each and every one was almost unbearable.

For both my daughter and me, our separations from family were—and still are—magnified by the distance between Australia and England. I had put us in a situation where we would never have all our loved ones easily accessible, where celebrations would always be missing someone and where 'home' was in two places.

For me, the worst separations of all were the times when I couldn't access the deeper reality that I'd known in moments of deep meditation and heightened consciousness. That seemed to be the most fundamental and awful separation of all. Perhaps it is what we are all missing.

Tagore beautifully captures the yearning and separation that runs in the veins of humanity:

It is the pang of separation that spreads throughout the world
and gives birth to shapes innumerable in the infinite sky.
It is this sorrow of separation that gazes in silence all night

> *from star to star and becomes lyric among rustling leaves in rainy darkness of July.*
>
> *It is this overspreading pain that deepens into loves and desires, into sufferings and joys in human homes; and this it is that ever melts and flows in songs through my poet's heart.*[70]

From the separation anxiety of an infant taken from its mother to the broken hearts of failed love affairs to the broken bonds of death, life's biggest struggles seem to be the situations that take us from unity and merging to separateness, potential isolation and loneliness.

People are typically drawn to situations where they can transcend the focus on their separate sense of self and are dissolved into a sense of 'oneness'. This can take all sorts of forms, from becoming absorbed in a natural environment or creative endeavour to blurring the edges with alcohol. It can be devotion to a humanitarian cause or being part of a crowd at a rock concert.

For some people—and I am one of them—sex isn't only about physical pleasure but also about merging and transcending self, becoming one with another and with the universe, if only for brief moments.

Love, the sort of love where one is totally merged and united with the beloved, is the essence of every fairy tale, which I think I always endeavoured to reach in my romantic relationships. While I occasionally touched that exquisite transcendent unity for a while, the pinnacle was frustratingly fleeting as separate selves battled on with life circumstances, and sometimes with each other.

All of these situations though can give a sense of returning to oneness beyond the duality of 'me and other' or subject and object.

Psychology tells us that we need an individuated self with clear boundaries to have healthy relationships.

Evolutionary theory tells us we have a primal fear of being alone because it makes us physically vulnerable in a world of sabre tooth tigers.

Well-meaning advisors tell us we can be alone without being lonely.

Yet still the moments that typically give our lives greatest significance are the ones where we are not just an island but reach out to another human being—family, lover, friend or stranger—or feel our oneness with nature or as part of a bigger cause.

Our separation is essential to becoming a functioning human being and has many uses in navigating the world but tends to pull us away from the open observation of simply seeing without naming; of being pure consciousness, through which different unnamed patterns, colours, sounds and sensations unfold.

Our education and schooling continue to emphasise bringing focused attention to specific elements of our environment so we can analyse and manipulate them, and communicate them in language. That is all very well in balance but predisposes most of us in current civilisation to focus on specifics divorced from their context.

Academic and scientific specialisation narrows perspective down to an even more discreet field and produces thought-leaders who genuinely cannot see beyond a limited area of separate pieces, mechanics and functions.

We see the design on the rug but rarely pull back from the detail to see the totality.

Along with our early attempts to identify parts of the world, we are introduced to 'good' and 'bad', 'like' and 'don't like' on which we build a lifelong division of our experience and create castles of our opinions.

Rather than simply experiencing what is, we divide into things we want more of and less of; things we agree with and disagree with. This all reinforces the self-concept and sets up constant striving to achieve some things and avoid others.

This increasingly conceptual, intellectual, busy-brain world has led to a human experience where most of us are one step removed most of the time from the reality that we are actually experiencing. Language, concepts and thinking about ourselves as objects all create a veil of separation between us and the pure reality of our experience.

Tibetan Llama, Chögyam Trungpa, says, "Labelling phenomena creates a feeling of a solid and definite world of things. Such a solid world reassures us that we are a solid continuous thing as well".[71]

So, our development and linguistic overlay predisposes us to see things as separate, clunky objects. Most of all we see ourselves as a separate subject pitted against the objects and other people of the world, managing them in whatever ways we are temperamentally inclined to—control, coercion, manipulation, passivity or cooperative endeavour.

Wittgenstein said, "The limits of my language mean the

limits of my world," and there are some interesting anthropological examples showing this in action.

In his book *Don't Sleep There Are Snakes,* Daniel Everett relates his time with the Piraha tribe whose language has no comparatives (e.g. bigger, smaller, biggest, smallest), no colour words, no numbers and no plurals. Their communication is almost always related only to the present moment—the immediate experience.

Their linguistic structure and convention of communication leave little possibility for abstract thought, speculation or analysis. Perhaps it is no coincidence that they are happy people!

> *Pirahas laugh about everything. They laugh at their own misfortune: when someone's hut blows over in a rainstorm, the occupants laugh more loudly than anyone. They laugh when they catch a lot of fish. They laugh when they catch no fish. They laugh when they're full and they laugh when they're hungry.*[72]

The conceptualisation and reification process is subtle and pervasive. Those on a spiritual path can just as easily fall into the same trap. As A.H. Almaas points out, "Something similar can happen to those who work exclusively with a non-dual perspective about reality: at some point, they begin to reify non-duality, and it becomes for them an object to aspire to and reach".

Whether we are a reality TV star building an empire or a renunciate searching for God, we continually tinker with our lives trying to manipulate circumstances to reach that elusive point of 'lasting happiness' or 'enlightenment' or to resolve feelings of emptiness, pointlessness or non-specific anguish.

The ideas of a paradise we have lost or a heaven we will return to are poignant myths that resonate with our sense that we have somehow become separated from a more blissful existence.

The garden of Eden in the Bible is a wonderful metaphor for this. Having created a perfect paradise for man and woman, God commands them not to eat of the tree of knowledge:

> *And the Lord God commanded the man, saying, 'Of every tree of the garden thou mayest freely eat: but of the tree of the knowledge of good and evil, thou shalt not eat of it: for in the day that thou eatest thereof thou shalt surely die'.*[73]

When the serpent comes, he stresses to Eve that the knowledge of good and evil will be a transformative step.

> *And the serpent said unto the woman, 'Ye shall not surely die: for God doth know that in the day ye eat thereof, then your eyes shall be opened, and ye shall be as gods, knowing good and evil'.*

Why is knowing about good and evil such a big deal? It remains what many religions, including Christianity, are based on so why would God try to keep humankind from this knowledge?

Here we have a story showing that dividing existence into conceptual parts and duality is what banishes us from the bliss of a unified perspective. The knowledge and consciousness that makes us as gods also brings our self-consciousness. This is indicated symbolically in the story by the fact that Adam and Eve suddenly realised that they were naked.

Self-consciousness brings trouble as well as possibility and we become aware of our own bodily death.

God tells Adam and Eve the implications: "In sorrow shalt thou eat of it all the days of thy life; thorns also and thistles shall it bring forth to thee".

With self-consciousness and duality, Adam and Eve are banished from Eden and a cherubim is put to guard the gate so that they may not enter to eat from the tree of life, which would give them immortality.

> *And the Lord God said, Behold, the man is become as one of us, to know good and evil: and now, lest he put forth his hand, and take also of the tree of life, and eat, and live for ever...*
>
> *So, he drove out the man; and he placed at the east of the garden of Eden cherubims, and a flaming sword which turned every way, to keep the way of the tree of life.*

As a child, it was easy to interpret this story as a test of Adam and Eve's obedience and the punishment of a father God when disobeyed, but any thinking adult must wonder why the tree of knowledge is such a crucial factor in humankind's mythological history. And what is this tree of life that confers immortality that we can no longer reach because of eating from the tree of knowledge?

In Catholicism this was the 'Original Sin' we all carry.

The fall from the grace of non-duality to separateness, and dividing the world into good and bad, do indeed set us up for all our problems and for our sense of being cast out.

Our knowledge of duality and our self-consciousness continue to both make us as gods yet bar us from some pre-existing state of bliss. Perhaps they also bar us from a life-perspective beyond our time-bound bodies, where we live forever.

There are times I have watched a beautiful sunset, wondered at a mountain view or stood on the ocean shore with a complex emotion of awe, pleasure and yearning. It's as if I want to penetrate the essence of what is there, to sustain the fleeting moment. The separation from it is both painful but inevitable in giving the joy of conscious observation.

That feeling has a close relation in the Japanese term 'mono no aware'—the bitter-sweetness of transience.

This is our lives. The separation and transience are qualities inherent in living as thinking, self-conscious, time-bound selves. Our moments of transcendence remind us that this is not all we are.

Separation is our greatest anguish but is also essential for us to be able to observe and know consciousness and live individual lives. Our separation brings our individual world into existence.

If we remained as part of the oneness with no awareness of individual being—like a very young baby—there would be consciousness but no objectified awareness of that consciousness and no ability to reflect.

Einstein said, "A human being is a part of the whole, called by us 'universe', a part limited in time and space. He experiences himself, his thoughts and feelings as separate from the rest—a kind of optical delusion of his consciousness".[74]

Pascal, the French mathematician, physicist and theologian, had a similar perspective. He said, "Our soul is cast into a body, where it finds number, time, dimension. Thereupon it reasons and calls this nature, necessity, and can believe nothing else".[75]

Darryl Reanney in *Music of the Mind* says, "Time is the illusion and unity, the profound insight that 'All is One', is the truth of the universe".

If we have tasted that truth and then lose it, our yearning is intense.

As Rabindranath Tagore expresses it:

> *Oh, dip my emptied life into that ocean, plunge it into the deepest fullness. Let me for once feel that lost sweet touch in the allness of the universe.*[76]

Rabia, one of the earliest recorded Islamic Sufi mystics, a woman from a poor background in the 9th century CE, spoke of the love of God that is beyond description, "There is no in-between in a lover and his beloved. It is an utterance born from longing, a description from tasting. He who tastes, knows".

The businessman, who had an experience of God in the park, which was related earlier, begged Krishnamurti to tell him how to regain that perspective. "It was an experience that totally ravished my heart… I would give everything, my life and all my possessions, to live again in that world."

As Jesus said, "Again, the kingdom of heaven is like unto treasure hid in a field; the which when a man hath found, he hideth, and for joy thereof goeth and selleth all that he hath, and buyeth that field".[77]

But what sort of game is this? It's hard not to question why a totality of love, bliss and consciousness would participate in this game of hide-and-seek—why things would have unfolded so we perceived ourselves as separate and then tried to get back to God, whether in this world or in heaven.

My little red catechism asked. 'Why did God make me?' and gave the answer: 'God made me to know Him and love Him and serve Him in this world, and be happy with Him forever in the next'.

Even with knowledge of a non-dual way of being and the words of many masters, the logical part of my brain still asks 'Why?'

The mystery remains. There is no clear reason why there is something rather than nothing, why this whole universe exists, why consciousness doesn't remain blissfully at rest but splits itself into billions of bodies.

The Indian tradition says this life is a *lila* (play) of Brahman.

The Sufis say the purpose of creation is for God to know himself. "If a Sufi is asked 'what was the purpose of this creation?', he will say that the Knower, the only Knower, wanted to know Himself, and there was only one condition of knowing Himself, and that was to make Himself intelligible to His own Being."[78]

Popular Sufi poet, Rumi captures the thought in metaphor:

Reality replied: O prisoner of time,
I was a secret treasure of kindness and generosity,
and I wished this treasure to be known,
so I created a mirror: its shining face, the heart;
its darkened back, the world;
The back would please you if you've never seen the face.

A similar idea is expressed by the poet Shelley. "I am the eye with which the Universe beholds itself and knows itself divine."

Back in the Advaita Vedanta tradition, Nisagadatta Maharaj said, "As Absolute, I am timeless, infinite, and I am awareness, without being aware of awareness... Unless there is space and duration, I cannot be conscious of myself".

John Thornton, Associate Professor at Griffith University with decades of study of artificial intelligence and philosophy, responded in the following way when I asked him if he could relate to the theory of everything being one consciousness.

If you just have the universe, everything at one in its absolute entirety, what would it be conscious of? There's nothing for it to be conscious of because it already is everything. It seems to me that the way it works is you've got to have some sort of part that becomes conscious of the rest of it for there to be an experience at all. Otherwise, you've just got a sleeping God, haven't you?

And that sounds consistent with the Sufi view. And not entirely inconsistent with my red catechism.

It also makes sense of evolving levels in consciousness in the creatures of the world. We're not only evolving and replicating our genes as a purposeless exercise, but to develop consciousness and eventually the self-reflective capacities, to know ourselves for what we truly are.

16

THE DILEMMA OF THE DECISION-MAKER

The realisation of no-self and non-duality lifts a great burden from any being that thinks it is a separate self struggling in a heartless universe. It is especially freeing for anyone like me who has been part of a religion or culture where he or she has to be worthy to win God's love, enlightenment or a place in heaven!

As pure consciousness, each of us is part of God (or the Source or the Whole if you prefer a non-theological word). From the moment I really saw that, the intense searching and trying was at an end.

As Lalla, a 14th century poet from Kashmir wrote, "I, Lalla, went out far in search of Shiva, the omnipresent lord; having wandered, I found him in my own body, sitting in his house".[79]

It is a truth that has been seen by many mystics but declaring 'I am God' has always been a dangerous position!

Christian mystic Meister Eckhart said, "The soul is not like God, she is identical with him". He was tried as a heretic.

Sufi mystic Ibn Arabi said:

> *When you realise the mystery of Oneness with the Divine, you will know that you are none other than God and that you have always been and always will be beyond every time and place... The soul sees God in all beings but only because it is God who is looking. He is lover and beloved, seeker and sought.*

Ralph Waldo Emerson also shared the vision:

> *We live in succession, in division, in parts, in particles. Meantime within man is the soul of the whole; the wise silence; the universal beauty, to which each and every particle is equally related; the eternal ONE.*[80]

Nisagadatta Maharaj said, "What you seek is so near you that there is no place for a way".

The Kabbalah, the mystical text of Judaism, says, "Do not say 'This is a stone and not God.' God forbid! Rather all existence is God and the stone is a thing pervaded by divinity".

As profound as this realisation is, this Julia body-mind still has to decide what to have for breakfast, who to vote for in the election and whether she really needs another new scarf! She'll still have an aversion to medical procedures involving injections and scalpels, a preference for sunny climates, a love of Bruce Springsteen and Leonard Cohen, and a tendency to have a hopelessly untidy desk!

The answer, it seems, is to let this personal body-mind do what it thinks is best but without the mistaken belief that any one of these decisions is going to make me more or less of what I really am or more or less worthy to reach some heaven or enlightenment.

Returning to Ramesh Balsekar, the Indian teacher in Mumbai, who I mentioned earlier, I got a very clear perspective of this action without a self. One of the essentials of Ramesh's teaching was, 'There is no doer'.

His ideas took the no-self and non-dual ideas to their logical conclusion. If there is no ghost in the machine, every action is the result of the body-mind's genes, conditioning, inputs from the environment and a sequence of thoughts that came into our minds.

Did we choose any of those? Then how can we claim responsibility? How can we be proud? How can we be guilty? How can we feel superior or inferior? How can we judge another? Pride and guilt are both pointless indulgences of a phantom self that believes it acted.

This certainly removes the impetus behind much of our mental worrying and self-analysis and must make us question whether it is all empty noise in an empty vessel!

As Ramesh says, "Why does Gary think 'Gary' exists? Because he thinks 'he' does actions. If 'Gary' doesn't do anything—who is Gary?"[81]

Ramesh advised continuing to act *as if* you have free will but knowing there is no doer. Your organism will not suddenly decide to go out and murder or maim if that has not been its tendency before.

If you were previously ruthless in trying to get something for yourself, the realisation of no-self may well undermine the drive for grasping, grabbing, competing and battling others. The body will still have its natural needs but these are relatively simple.

> *In life you cannot live without making decisions, and my answer is to make decisions as if you have free will. Consider all the consequences and alternatives—then come to a decision. But deep down you know that the decision could not have been different from God's Will; otherwise that decision wouldn't have happened...*

So, I can only respond in the way I feel is best. Sometimes that achieves the outcome I hoped for and sometimes it doesn't. Many times in life, and certainly at death, the individual plan is derailed.

If we look very closely at how action arises, we can start to see through the illusion of an individual controller. A situation presents itself (events beyond my control). Thoughts of action come in (did I actually choose those thoughts or did they just arise?). I make a choice based on my world perspective (did I really choose that world perspective or has it grown from a mixture of inbuilt characteristics, environment, conditioning and further unbidden influences?). The outcome develops (sometimes what my self-concept hoped but sometimes not).

Any simplistic idea of a rational 'controller' making our decisions is also blown out of the water by Daniel

Kahneman, Nobel Prize winner in Economics, who explains the two systems at work in the brain. In *Thinking Fast and Slow*, he shows how flawed our perspectives can be and how many illusions shape our decisions, even when we attempt to take the logical course of action.

Through a mixture of intuition, logic, conditioning, need, moral code and environmental influence, I make a decision.

If the outcome is not what I hoped for, I tend to think I made the 'wrong' decision but that is a mind-created illusion that something else could have been done in that particular moment. However finally balanced a decision, all my inputs and perspectives at that moment led me to that decision—full stop.

Really understanding this perspective starts to build genuine compassion for others and for ourselves. It takes away the pride of 'I'm smarter than you because my life circumstances are better' or 'I'm more spiritual because I meditate every day'. It removes the self-righteousness of 'I would never do what she did' and the guilt of 'I did something awful that caused pain'.

Increasingly, there is a realisation that everybody is doing the best they can manage at that moment with the circumstances and perspective they have been given. And it's not that 'I' am being compassionate—there is compassion arising through seeing the truth of the situation.

Like Ramesh Balsekar, contemporary teacher A. H. Almaas says you cannot choose your experience completely since your experience is the result of the interaction between where you are and what is happening in the universe. "There is no such thing as being independent of the universe since you are part of it... If the universe is unfolding and you are part of the unfoldment, what to do becomes clear—you just go with it."[82]

There is a teaching story Ramana Maharshi told about our inability to stop striving. He said we are like a man who is used to walking everywhere, carrying his huge bag around with him. When one day he is given a train ticket and gets on a train, he cannot put his bag down because he cannot trust that the train will carry it for him.

And there is the famous biblical quote, "Look at the birds of the air, for they neither sow nor reap nor gather into barns; yet your heavenly Father feeds them. Are you not of more value than they? Which of you by worrying can add one cubit to his stature?"[83]

When we are operating from the perspective of duality and being a separate self, the opposites and struggle are inevitable. We all think we might be able to have happiness without sadness, pleasure without pain but that is a conceptual illusion.

In struggling to manipulate circumstances and our inner responses to get greater pleasure or merit or security, we typically writhe and wrench ourselves away from what is the innate perfection of every conscious moment.

The point is that most codes of behaviour, religious or secular, are built on the foundation of belief in a self that can be tinkered with and enhanced to achieve some conceptual perfection. And there's great satisfaction in feeling one is 'working towards enlightenment' or 'living a spiritual life' or 'becoming a better person' or 'waging God's war'.

We're always striving for a goal and the anticipation of greater satisfaction, greater bliss, greater peace, less suffering or more brownie points for 'the Big Beyond'.

And paradoxically, that tends to drag us away from the present moment—the only place where we can really know peace and joy by simply *being*.

The illusion of time and importance of 'now'—not only as a conceptual moment but also as a living reality—comes through from many of commentators who have experienced the deeper or mystical levels of consciousness. Our concepts of past and future are mental constructs that keep us in a dream. Reality is only now.

Schrödinger said, from the point of view of his scientific and philosophical explorations, "...mind is always *now*. There is really no before and after for mind. There is only a now that includes memories and expectations".[84]

Thich Nhat Hanh says, "Your true home is in the here and the now".

So, whether we want to get the most out of our life experience or enter a deeper state of consciousness, the living present moment is the key. The more we can come to that without a chattering self-concept and without conceptualising and worrying about past and future, the more real and intrinsically rich our life is.

Eckhart Tolle's popular book *Power of Now* has helped that truth resonate with a wider audience.

At its best, the current mindfulness movement is also offering a practice to make present-centred being a little easier.

Being present doesn't mean I can't plan a holiday when I need to or develop a menu for next Friday's dinner or even work towards a longer-term goal. Using the mind as a tool to work out what's practically needed is its natural function. The problem arises when I live in imagination of future or past events and my imaginary self's role in the scenario—and start to worry about what I did or what the outcome will be.

Should we not blame those who hurt us? Should we not blame and punish criminals? With this understanding, blame is not logical. Our justice systems should rather look to retrain the body-mind's thinking and to protect those that may be harmed by a body-mind that is violent or damages others.

If the actions of our body-mind have transgressed society's norms and laws, as a result of our unique genes and history, we need have no guilt. However, the body-mind may still have to bear the consequences. The consequences will depend on the cultural norms of our time and place—a fine, prison, divorce, job termination or beheading!

The wise body-mind will certainly still weigh up the risks of ignoring the rules and the effect its actions may have on others.

Without believing I am the doer, my body-mind will fulfil its role in the greater scheme of things like an actor in a movie. The only difference is that I've never been told the story or seen the full script so I don't fully understand the significance of my lines. There has to be a certain trust that the big picture is unfolding is as it should be—as it must.

I have the supposed free will to do whatever I want but I cannot control the outcomes. Thinking I can, or that I could have done differently or should have done differently, is all part of the illusion of being a self.

This understanding is not about total passivity. While struggling to achieve is usually rooted in belief in a separate self that has do something, there is also a lighter way of letting the body-mind do what's natural in the circumstances without taking credit or blame. Its genes and conditioning have created exactly what is needed for this unfolding drama!

As A.H. Almaas says in *Facets of Unity*, "If a truck is barrelling towards you on the freeway, enlightened action is neither letting it hit you or getting angry that the truck driver is endangering you… but moving out of the way".[85]

I think those who do something courageous to save someone's life are usually acting from that pure response without analysis and complex decision-making. They act spontaneously and 'selflessly' as we say.

It's also interesting that they frequently don't feel they are heroes and say, paradoxically, that they feel humbled by receiving a medal. Why does it humble them rather than make them proud?

I think it is because at some level they know they were not the doer in that moment. They were the conduit through which life acted. Perhaps, without realising it, they are trying to convey that they feel as if there is no self here on whom to pin a medal!

Similarly, many writers, musicians and artists often intuit that they cannot take personal credit; that their words appear in consciousness or an idea flows through them. Practicing their skills prepares the body to be even better at surrendering to the flow and being an instrument of expression rather than trying and forcing performance through personality.

We can all play our role as human beings according to our lights without guilt or regret.

What was greater ignorance in us must have given way to clearer consciousness for guilt to even arise. Our remorse shows we are a little less identified with an illusory personality and a little more identified with life around us.

The Buddha taught that there is no individual doer and that realising this is the doorway to enlightenment. "Suffering exists but no sufferer can be found. Actions exist but no doer of actions is there. Nirvana exists but no-one who enters it." [86]

The Bhagavad Gita has a similar perspective. "All actions take place in time by the interweaving of the forces of Nature; but the man lost in selfish delusion thinks that he himself is the actor".

The answer is not to reject the personal life and its activities but to see its operation as a relatively surface phenomenon. It is possible to see the swirls on the rug and see the whole rug simultaneously.

Even the try-hard, pesky seeker looking for enlightenment or God, is a part of the insubstantial and is like the wave that is looking for the ocean.

Ramesh says:

> *What is seeking? Seeking is 'you' wanting to know God. Whatever you know is an object and you are the subject. So, if you want to know God, what does it mean? You are the subject and God is the object, but what exists is the other way around. God is the Subject and you are the object. So how can an object know the Subject? ...Therefore, the more the seeker tries to find God, the more frustrated he becomes.*

The ultimate resolution, he says, is the realisation that there is no doer and no seeker.

> *And, if the one who wanted to know God has disappeared, then what has happened? . . . the one who wanted to know God has become God because God is all there is.*[87]

For me, more than 30 years of searching for God has, in one sense, been a wild-goose chase. I can see why there is so much paradox in teaching stories and why scientists would rather devote their time to looking for quarks!

As Ramesh said, "If you have the choice between enlightenment and a million dollars, take the million dollars! Because if you get the million dollars, there will be somebody there to enjoy the million dollars; but if you get enlightenment there's no one there to enjoy the enlightenment".

While Zen monks traditionally laugh when they 'get it', my dawning realisation leaves more of a sense of bemusement as it becomes increasingly clear that what I was searching for was here all the time and, in one sense, all the struggle was quite unnecessary and the seeker quite unreal!

Yet all the running around in circles has eventually exhausted this Julia-person so it stays quiet and dissolves into the deeper reality that it was always a part of. In that place, there is peace, gentle joy, love and wonder.

PART THREE

SPIRITUALITY FOR THE FUTURE

17

THE FIGHT FOR OUR SOULS

ARRIVING BACK IN INDIA in 2012 to gather my thoughts for this book, I want to draw together what I have learnt and how it fits into the big picture of life, the universe and everything.

I would like to show how spirituality is still relevant for humanity and totally compatible with science.

While scientists continue to look for the theory of everything, I want a theory of everything where science and spirituality both have equal stakes in the future, as they did in medieval times.

As Karen Armstrong points out in *The Case for God,* science and religion weren't always at war but were two sides of humanity's quest and exploration. "Today it is often assumed that modern science has always clashed with religion. Kepler, a mathematician of extraordinary genius reminds us that early modern science was rooted in faith."[88]

Psychiatrist and polymath Ian McGilchrist also calls for

a more balanced approach in his book *The Master and his Emissary*. He says, "There is a tendency for the life sciences to consider a mechanistic universe more 'real', even though physics long ago moved away from the legacy of nineteenth century materialism …".[89]

I start my journey in Kerala. It's an interesting mixture from a religious point of view because it has a large Christian population in a country of predominantly Hindu and Muslim people. As my taxi bumps along pot-holed roads in the late-evening darkness, I notice the many churches with reminders of the saints of my Catholic childhood—St Anthony's, St Francis, St Thomas, St Joseph's…

Lying on my bed next morning in a little guest house in Cochin, I can hear a school band playing 'Onward Christian Soldiers'. Like the churches, it seems oddly out of place but the Christians have been trying to get their market share of souls here since the 6th century CE.

The remarkable thing about India is that, whether Christian, Hindu, Muslim, Sikh or Jain, most people have a very vibrant relationship with the spiritual aspect of their lives.

Whereas, in the west, science and materialism have eroded religious belief, in India the gods and goddesses seem to have retained their power even in a scientifically-explained universe. They are petitioned and thanked in even the most materialistic ventures.

In the little shop where I go to find out about an Indian SIM card, the image of goddess Laxmi has pride of place behind the counter amongst mobile phone accessories, cigarettes and batteries.

There is hardly an auto-rickshaw, taxi, bus, shop or restaurant that isn't displaying its owner's chosen god or guru, whether Ganesh, Jesus, Sai Baba, Shiva, St Anthony, Kali, Durga, Virgin Mary or Guru Nanak. The exceptions are the Muslim taxi drivers who do not show images of Mohammed but may have a quotation from the Koran.

These images represent a powerful impulse in humanity to believe in 'the divine' and I wonder if the majority in the west have rejected it at their own peril.

Whereas a couple of hundred years ago, we too might have seen ourselves as 'made in the image of God' but standing in humility before Him, we now see ourselves as a 'soft machine' driven by survival genes in a world created by material processes and chance.

The rejection of anything beyond mechanical materialism has gathered pace since Darwin shook any simplistic literal view of the biblical creation process, and contemporary atheists such as Richard Dawkins, Christopher Hitchens and Daniel Dennett are loud voices we can't ignore.

They have arguments in two areas—one is that the evidence of evolution and science leaves no need for 'God'; the other is that religions are for primitive, childlike people and have caused much mayhem in the world.

In *The Selfish Gene,* Richard Dawkins refers to us as 'survival machines' and the very title of the book anthropomorphises human biological processes with a descriptor that legitimises a 'survival of the fittest' life approach. In *The God Delusion,* he sets up an argument between evolution and creationism and concludes that, "All available evidence (and there is a vast amount of it) favours evolution". [90]

These atheists view everything very simplistically in black and white, 'either-or' terms and they seem to genuinely believe they are doing humanity a favour by trying to rid it of God. They only consider the most literal interpretations of God and confuse the basic issue with a smokescreen of the atrocities committed by religions over the ages.

The confusion is inherent in the title of Christopher Hitchens' best-selling book *God is Not Great: How Religions Poison Everything.* The greatness of God cannot be disputed by the ignorance of humans who are manipulated by divisive religious leaders.

Hitchens seems blind to the fact that his attitudes buy into the same divisiveness that sets up religious battlegrounds. He is not looking for a shared understanding but for a fight with religion. His disdain for his fellow humans is obvious in comments like, "I leave it to the faithful to burn each other's churches and mosques and synagogues, which they can always be relied upon to do". [91]

The average person hasn't got the time, inclination or background to read each new scientific book that emerges and consider its arguments carefully. Instead we are spoon-fed small conclusions and big speculations in news snippets or sound-bites that all add up to a picture of ourselves as cuddly robots in a vast accidental universe.

The media often buys into the scientific viewpoint without intelligent questions.

Even respected newspapers like Britain's *Observer* run headlines like 'Science is just one gene away from defeating religion'[92] above an article that does absolutely nothing to support that assertion with evidence. The article turns out to be a general discussion about Darwinism and Dawkinism that justifies its headline by leaving the reader with the thought, "When we understand how our brains generate religious ideas, and what the Darwinian adaptive value of such brain processes is, what will be left for religion?"

Similar to genetic scientists and physicists demystifying our origins, denying the possibility of God and reducing us to mechanical-chemical soup, those working in the neuroscience field are reducing our mind, consciousness and behaviour to nothing more than bio-chemical brain processes driven by genetic predispositions.

Pioneer of artificial intelligence, Marvin Minsky sums it up when he says that the human mind is a computer made of meat.

I am fascinated by the work that biologists and neuroscientists are doing but I also find some of their conclusions blinkered and depressing.

While I don't doubt that much of their work has the material mechanisms right, the assumption that we are *only* this seems an arrogant framework within which to work. Even if you can fix a TV or change the channel by moving wires, or destroy it by smashing it, you will have missed an essential element of its nature if you don't understand that it is a receiving apparatus.

While philosophers might be able to help us, most of

them are also caught up in strict logic and tend to tangle us in mental acrobatics rather than shedding any real light on our dilemma.

Philosophy has set rules of argument and engagement that can be a straightjacket for anyone wanting a deeper experiential insight. The discipline of epistemology establishes rules for what we can know and how we know it, what constitutes proof and how to win a philosophical debate.

Academics like Owen Flanagan, Professor of Philosophy at Duke University, seem genuinely surprised that people are not satisfied by this approach. Flanagan says in *The Really Hard Problem—Meaning in a Material World*, "Ordinary well-educated folk know little about epistemology. It is a common experience to teach the cosmological or design arguments to bright undergraduates and show that they are invalid; only to have students say they still believe in God because of those very arguments". [93]

Logically, philosophers may be able to prove God doesn't exist, or at least that we can explain existence and live a good life without the necessity for God, but they offer little for hungry souls. As Pascal said, "The end point of rationality is to demonstrate the limits of rationality".

Paul Feyerabend (1924-1994), Professor of Philosophy at University of California, cautioned that all ideologies, including science, must be seen in perspective. He argued that science has now become as oppressive as the ideologies it once had to fight and that scientific heretics are not tolerated in much the same way that religious heretics were once ostracised.

He said the fact they are not killed has more to do with society's progress than with science's tolerance. "Heretics in science are still made to suffer from the *most severe* sanctions this relatively tolerant civilisation has to offer."[94]

The rules for operating outside the straightjackets of science or philosophy are not clear and it's easy to see why most academics have little time for the nebulous world of belief and inner exploration. The obvious difficulty in achieving any constructive dialogue is that science likes to think it operates by logic alone while traditional mystical paths are very clear that logical thinking is not the way to approach an understanding or experience of God.

In the meantime, the average man or woman is left with a diminished sense of their own worth and may be encouraged to live life as the selfish animal that science is telling us we are.

Our religions are not only under attack from the vocal atheists but also the secular humanists and philosophers who are attempting to wrest the moral and ethical ground from religious hands. They want to establish life-meaning in human good, human happiness and progress, without reference to any spiritual or religious paradigm.

Alain de Botton's *Religion for Atheists: A Non-believer's Guide to the Uses of Religion* epitomises this attitude, arguing that religion is useful and packed with good ideas and insights on how we might live and arrange our societies, build a sense of community, make relationships last, overcome feelings of envy and inadequacy, inspire travel, get more out of art, and reconnect with the natural world. Everything, in fact, except undertake a personal search for truth and meaning, or experience something beyond, or deeper than, our personal reality.

Owen Flannigan, mentioned above, is a tolerant sort of atheist who is prepared to allow the usefulness of some traditionally spiritual disciplines such as mindfulness and meditation. Despite his great depth of logical argument and his obvious goodwill to humanity, reading his *The Really Hard Problem—Meaning in a Material World* is in many ways a superficial experience that never really resonates with a longing for meaning.

I feel there's a real danger emerging from these well-meaning secular humanists suggesting we can have all the benefits and 'good bits' from the religious traditions without any self-sacrifice or deeper awareness. Having never experienced the totally re-orienting result of deeper spiritual connection, they dismiss the desire for it as a childish wish or a biological need that had an adaptive use somewhere in our evolution.

Perhaps it's not surprising in our demanding world that mindfulness and meditation are also being relegated to a commoditised tool—something to fit in your lunch-break between your bikini-wax appointment, gym work-out and cocktail hour.

Of course, any small taste is better than nothing but the emphasis on these techniques as de-stressors so one can continue to live at a super-fast speed to pursue material enhancement and a self-story fails to acknowledge their more serious purpose and potential.

What were once sacred techniques have become secular tools to prop up the ego that is threatening to crack under the pressure of relentless activity separated from conscious life context and from the grounding aspects of a natural environment.

Where once meditation was a technique to go beyond the self within a spiritual discipline, now it is often used as to enhance the self and add to one's list of experiences. Walk the Inca trail—tick. Backpack in Costa Rica—tick. Sky-dive in the Seychelles—tick. Meditate in the Himalayas—tick.

I hope some of the people who participate in meditation or mindfulness do get the message 'there is something more to this' rather than thinking, 'I've been there, done that, got my burst of alpha waves and really reduced my stress levels'.

My Indian taxi driver stops to buy marigolds for the Ganesh on his dashboard before he takes me to my destination and two neatly-uniformed Indian schoolgirls with long plaits push open the door of an ornate church across the street. There are smiles on their faces that I don't often see in the west.

It's one of the things that draws me back to India. Despite plenty of horrendous craziness here, there is still a tangible connection to the divine and usually (give or take a few notably brutal moments in history) room for everyone to express that in their own way.

Most in India take very seriously the concept of *darshan*—a sight or glimpse of the divine. It can come at different times but is especially likely at auspicious places and when one comes to the temple on auspicious days.

A few weeks after leaving Kerala, I arrive in Tiruchirappalli and find the Vaikunta Ekadasi festival is about to take place.

At the great Sri Ranganathaswamy Temple, one of India's biggest temple complexes, extra police contingents from around Tamil Nadu state, bomb disposal squads and traffic control officers have been drafted in to deal with the huge crowds.

The *Hindu Times* runs a special 8-page broadsheet festival supplement including the 108 names of Vishnu and explains: "In Vaikunta Ekadasi, it is hard to decipher whether the Lord adores the devout or vice versa as the dividing line is blurred, drawing the devout to the god even as it brings divinity to earth".

From 4am, queues start to form in the temple complex and, when I visit mid-morning, I am told the queue will take 2-3 hours to reach the inner sanctum where the devotees pay homage to Vishnu.

Non-Hindus are not allowed into the inner sanctum so I am spared the long shuffle through the temple courtyards in blazing sun and stifling humidity.

Once again, I am aware how deeply committed Indians are to their religious faith and the extreme physical discomforts and deprivations they will endure in the spirit of pilgrimage. These are ordinary Indians—often whole families of all ages—who will queue or sacrifice themselves in a way people in the west now only do for tickets to an iconic rock star or to grab the cheapest TV at the Boxing Day sales.

A young man standing next to me asks the usual question

'What country you are coming from?' and explains the festival. "People are waiting for a glimpse of God. For us this festival is like the gates of Heaven open for a moment and we can see God."

"Do *you* see God?" I ask, wondering if a well-educated, English-speaking Indian is able to glimpse God in the temple.

He gives an enigmatic Indian head nod and I am no wiser.

18

QUANTUM PHYSICS BESIDE THE TEMPLE

I AM ON A SLEEPER-TRAIN to Madurai, in one of six bunks in a cramped shared carriage with four men and a nun. I've swapped my top bunk for a middle one as the contortions to climb the wooden ladder and wriggle between the foot of the bunk and the ceiling require superior gymnastic ability, which I've never been blessed with!

I've set my alarm clock for 2am when the train is due in Madurai. Somehow, I extricate myself and my too-large bag from the shared cupboard-like space in the near darkness and stumble off the train at the right station. I pass shrouded sleeping bodies in the station entrance and find an autorickshaw to whisk me through the almost deserted streets to a hotel within ear-shot of the railway.

Madurai is the home of one of South India's largest and most magnificent temple complexes and I'm keen to visit this ancient site, which is still a vibrant place of meaning for the people here.

In between exploring the town, I am reading *Quantum Physics for Poets* trying to better understand this important branch of science.

In some ways, it may seem that Indian temples and quantum physics couldn't be further apart, sitting at two ends of a spectrum of superstition and leading-edge science, but they have more in common than we first imagine.

Apart from the fact that the idea of atoms dates back to the *Vaisheshika* beliefs in India over two thousand years ago, it is in quantum physics that we find a link between consciousness and matter and where we may be able to integrate some of the mystical perspective with science.

The mechanistic, predictable, cause-and-effect science that still underpins most scientific thinking was first shown to have a nasty rip in its armour over a century ago. While I don't claim to have major expertise in quantum theory, I believe it is an important part of the debate.

It doesn't give us 'God' in the traditional Abrahamic sense but it shows consciousness has a role in creating matter and it defies the boundaries of distance as we know them.

Quantum mechanics studies the interaction of energy and matter at the level of atoms and sub-atomic particles. Scientists became aware in the late 19th century that they were seeing phenomena that couldn't be explained by classical physics, and Max Planck developed his first quantum theory in 1900. The groundwork continued through the early 20th century, culminating in the Copenhagen interpretation in the late 1920s, which set the foundation for continuing exploration.

Neils Bohr, one of the important scientists involved, famously said, "If quantum mechanics hasn't profoundly shocked you, you haven't understood it yet".

Because the principles of quantum mechanics are complex, often counter-intuitive and not easily accessible, their significance is still not widely understood. Yet this relatively young branch of physics has made possible many of the high-tech inventions of recent decades from transistors to lasers, from nuclear reactors to the microchip, from MRI machines to the internet.

From the perspective of this book, the basic principles of quantum theory take us beyond the old physics to one where consciousness can affect matter—and where divisions between consciousness and matter may break down altogether.

A central facet of the theory is that matter at the sub-atomic level has the properties of both particles and waves. This is called 'wave-particle duality'.

The wave function of matter can be described mathematically as the probability the object will be found in any location where it is measured. But the key point is that *the act of observing or measuring causes the matter to change from a wave of possibility to a particle.*

From among all the possible wave locations, the matter temporarily becomes a particle in a single location. This is known as the 'collapse of the wave function'.

As Amit Goswami, theoretical nuclear physicist at University of Oregon Institute for Theoretical Physics, says, "If we follow this thinking, it means that without consciousness there is no collapse, no material particles, no materiality".[95]

As if that isn't enough of a revelation to ponder, quantum mechanics has another big one: the principle of 'quantum entanglement'.

Quantum entanglement says that two or more related quantum objects remain related across distance and continue to react in complementary ways, even where there is no possibility for communication to pass between them.

For instance, if observing one wave causes it to collapse as a particle with 'spin up' the other entangled object will simultaneously collapse with 'spin down' even if it is a huge distance away.

In 2017, *Science* magazine reported that Chinese scientists had demonstrated this effect over greater distances than ever before. The experiment by a group of Chinese researchers, led by Professor Jian-Wei Pan of the Chinese Academy of Sciences (CAS), used a satellite orbiting at between 500 and 2,000 kilometres above Earth, to direct beams of entangled photon pairs at telescopes up to 1,203 kilometres apart.[96]

When the photons were received, Professor Lu and his colleagues were able to demonstrate that, despite the distance between them, the individual photons at each location were still entangled with their counterparts at the other ground station.

Here we have, in the very foundation of matter, a connection between things that needs no communication or obvious means of influence to affect a change.

Einstein resisted the findings of quantum mechanics, which he called 'spooky action at a distance'. For particles to instantly communicate in some way across vast distances would breach his theory that nothing can travel faster than the speed of light.

Quantum physicist David Bohm explained this feature of 'non-locality' by speculating that at the quantum level, locations no longer exist. All points in space are equal to all other points in space and it is meaningless to speak of things as separate.

Like Einstein, Schrödinger, who jointly won the Nobel Prize for Physics with Dirac in 1933 for his work on atomic theory, was initially a sceptic. He developed his famous 'cat in a box' thought experiment to show the flaws of applying the microscopic principles at a macroscopic level.

In his hypothetical situation, you have a cat shut in a box with a flask of lethal gas that can be activated by the decay of a single radioactive particle. The decay of radioactive particles is unpredictable but the small amount in this experiment has a 50 percent chance of decaying within an hour and setting off the mechanism that would smash the flask of gas and kill the cat.

If we apply the observer principle of quantum physics, we express it that the cat is half alive and half dead until the observer opens the box and finds it to be one way or the other.

Although this experiment claimed to highlight the incongruity of quantum theory saying that a system can be simultaneously in different states until an observation is made, later research has confirmed that quantum theory can actually lead to mixed states at a macroscopic level.

Like the other big gaps in scientific understanding, the 'why' of quantum behaviour is still unsolved. As Lederman and Hill say in *Quantum Physics for Poets,* "Physicists have brilliantly deciphered how quantum theory works but they are only clerks taking dictation or workers on an assembly line when it comes to trying to understand *why* it is this way".

The weirdness of quantum mechanics opens up many speculative arguments including the theory of parallel universes—one universe where the cat in the box is dead and one where it is alive! Or one universe where I separated from Ellis and made a life in Australia and another where I stayed in England with whatever consequences unfolded from that.

It seems to me that it is no more fanciful to speculate that entanglement and the collapse of waves into particles may connect us all in the ongoing creation of this universe.

If conscious observation can affect matter, maybe those studying consciousness have things reversed. Instead of brain activity creating consciousness, perhaps consciousness is creating brain activity.

If the link between entangled particles is beyond communication in time, perhaps all matter has an aspect outside of the dimension of time.

David Bohm demonstrates how this could be in his ingenious example of a fish tank full of fish being simultaneously filmed by two TV cameras on two adjoining sides of the tank. The two images are transmitted to two separate TV screens.

An observer of these two representations in two dimensions might see there is a relationship between the two—a fish that swims towards the viewer on one screen reappears at a different angle on the other—but there is no obvious causality between the two because the three-dimensional source is not seen.

He suggests that the non-local, non-causal relationship of quantum elements can be seen in a similar way as a projection of a reality with more dimensions, or 'three dimensional projections of six-dimensional reality'.

Another of Bohm's ideas that may be relevant to how our universe functions is that of the hologram.

Karl Pribram, professor of psychology and cognitive neuroscience at Georgetown University explains the hologram simply. He says that, if you have a movie projector projecting an image on a white screen and you remove the lens, you see only a blur of scattered light. But, if you place your glasses between the projector and the light, you get two identical versions of the image on the screen. If you hold up 100 lenses, you would get 100 images on the screen. He says, "Patterns that seem to be irretrievably annihilated are in fact still present in every portion of the scattered light".[97]

David Bohm observed that if we did not have telescopes and other lenses to observe the universe, it would appear to us as a hologram; that the structure of the background radiation of the universe is holographic. Pribram points out that the lens of our eyes may perform a similar function to a projector lens in creating an image from a scattered source.

This hologram concept and its alignment with many unexplained phenomena is explored in much greater depth in Michael Talbot's book *The Holographic Universe,* which was originally published in 1991 and reissued in 2011. I came upon this book late in my research and found he had already digested and clearly explained much of the physics I had laboriously researched and tried to piece together.

While some of his speculations will remain in the 'what if?' category, they are grounded in the work of Bohm and Pribram and feature fascinating historical cases of events outside our usual expectations of how reality works.

Michael Talbot died aged 38 from Chronic Lymphocytic Leukemia, which was a loss to the greater debate on science and 'spiritual' reality.

These perspectives from quantum mechanics must surely open our minds to a reality that has many possibilities currently beyond our limited, cause-and-effect science.

I know scientists get very annoyed when 'quantum' is applied to healing and all sorts of half-baked theories but there is no denying that consciousness has a role that wasn't even conceived of until the twentieth century. Reality may yet prove to be more incredible than anything our myths can conceive or our minds can grasp.

It seems logical to me that our minds may have the specific function of *reducing* what we can grasp by *limiting* input.

Perhaps to operate in this world and make sense of it, there has to be a brain tuned to a particular channel. When we transcend normal perception, through drugs, meditation, spontaneous revelation or brain damage, we may by-pass that limiting filter. Then we see either another channel or more of the background that is invisible with our normal focus.

There's a glimpse of how this might be the possible in the

book *My Stroke of Insight* by Jill Bolte Taylor. Jill documents the stroke that all but wiped out the left hemisphere of her brain. After the shattering event, she found her life instantly switched from a focus on 'doing' to a state of 'being'. This was not only because she was confined to a hospital bed but because her whole perception had changed.

She recalls that the urgency of time-consciousness had disappeared and things looked very different. She stopped feeling like a small separate entity with boundaries and felt enormous and expansive. She lost her ability to think in language, or to consider past or future so was held in the present moment. She says, "All I could perceive was right here, right now, and it was beautiful… It was impossible for me to distinguish the physical boundaries between objects because everything radiated with similar energy".[98]

She says that, despite her neurological trauma, an unforgettable sense of peace and calm pervaded her being. In that state, she also had a different perspective on 'self'. As she expressed it, "For all these years of my life, I really had been a figment of my own imagination!"

For a while she lived in a state where the painful hell of a wounded body failing to interact with the external world co-existed with "heaven… in a consciousness that soared in eternal bliss".

While living with only half a brain makes normal life virtually impossible, and Jill had a long road back to managing ordinary things, it shows that our 'normal' view of reality has its own built-in limitation on other possible perspectives.

19

ONENESS IN DIVERSITY

PARADOXICALLY, INDIA THE HOME of *Advaita Vedanta,* is also the place where the multiplicity of creation is at its most vivid and diverse.

On the streets of Madurai, as in many India cities, there is sensory overload. In one short walk from my hotel, there are men with barrows of marigold and jasmine garlands, a random procession with drums banging and trumpets playing, and an elephant adorned with decorative patterns. There's an old woman begging, stalls with bright clothes made by the local tailors, an electronics shop blasting Bollywood music, and the constant toot-toot of autorickshaws. The smell of spices from a busy canteen-like restaurant mingles with the stench of open drains and exhaust fumes.

Not least of all, there's the continuous human river that spills through every thoroughfare—an ever-colourful and ever-changing flow of young, old, beautiful, disfigured, desperate, joyful, smiling, graceful, conniving, friendly and hopeful.

How are we conscious of the dance of atoms as all these separate patterns in the kaleidoscope of life?

I'm confident that, in the not-too-distant future, the *Advaita Vedanta* philosophy of non-duality and the understanding of quantum theory may be seen more widely as complementary worldviews that allow us to understand our consciousness and the unity that underlies diversity.

Edwin Schrödinger, of the cat experiment, said, "Quantum physics reveals a basic oneness of the universe".

In the book *One Mind,* Larry Dossey devotes a number of pages to Schrödinger and the development of his world view, which combined his scientific knowledge with the philosophy of Schopenhauer and inspiration from the Upanishads.

While Schrödinger was not religious or saintly, he was convinced that there is only one consciousness underlying the millions of human minds. He said, "The multiplicity is only apparent; in truth there is only one mind".[99]

He also believed consciousness is infinite in space and time, therefore eternal and immortal.

David Bohm said, "Both observer and observed are merging and interpenetrating aspects of one whole reality, which is indivisible and unanalysable".[100]

He emphasised that relativity and quantum theory agree, in that they both imply the need to look on the world as an undivided whole, in which all parts of the universe, including the observer and his instruments, merge and unite in one totality. "Thus, the classical idea of the separability of the world into distinct but interacting parts is no longer valid or relevant. Rather we have to regard the universe as *an undivided and unbroken whole.*"

Speculating how we could account for the anomalies of quantum physics, he says that the universe—and however many other universes—may be like an ocean of enfoldment and unfoldment. We only see limited dimensions of this, not the interconnectedness.

He gives an example that likens it to a thick glycerine gel contained between two glass cylinders of differing size—the smaller inside the larger. A drop of ink inserted in the gel would appear as a point or solid particle. If you then twist the outer cylinder, the ink would disperse in a long, twisted trail. The molecules of the drop would stay connected even when they were dispersed. The action could be reversed to reform a distinct droplet with a reverse twist action.

He explains that what we call empty space contains an immense background of energy and that matter as we know it is a small, wavelike excitation on top of this background. It is rather like a tiny ripple on a vast sea. "The things that appear to our senses are derivative form and their true meaning can be seen only when we consider the plenum, in which they are generated and sustained, and into which they must ultimately vanish."

In his book *Biocentrism,* Robert Lanza offers a similar scientific theory, which also aligns beautifully with the mystical perspective. He proposes that, rather than being a belated and minor outcome after billions of years of lifeless physical processes, life and consciousness are absolutely fundamental to our understanding of the universe.

His argument is that consciousness is the key to everything and that the common perception that we are dealing with a solid universe 'out there' is the error.

He says, "Nothing is perceived but the perceptions themselves and nothing exists outside of consciousness".

This can be also demonstrated at a classical science level. In physics, there are no independent shapes and colours to be seen but only as an experience created in the observer by photons passing through the retina.

It is also demonstrated by the old riddle, "Does the tree falling in the forest make a sound if there's no-one to hear it?"

The simple answer is 'no', because the sound waves created are only waves until they reach an ear-drum attached to a brain and consciousness.

John Thornton, Associate Professor researching artificial intelligence at Griffith University, who we met earlier relating a mushroom-induced experience in his youth, says:

> *The experience you're having isn't an experience of the neurons firing. It's an experience of the meaning of the form that the neurons have captured. And consciousness is the means of turning what's going on in the brain into an experience of the world. So, it's doing something extraordinary, but it's not cause and effect... Consciousness, if you like, is the power that makes the world.*

Looking at the deeper level of subatomic particles, Lanza says that the behaviour of all objects and particles is inextricably linked to the presence of an observer. Without the presence of a conscious observer, they only exist in an undetermined state of probability waves.

He agrees with Bohm and sounds more like one of the mystics when he says, "In truth there can be no break between the observer and the observed. If the two are split, the reality is gone".

He also makes the point that, if one travels at speeds approaching the speed of light, both time and distance change. Someone travelling just below the speed of light would see a year pass on their watch but 520 centuries would have passed back on earth. If one could travel at the full speed of light, one would find oneself everywhere in the universe at once. And, if a photon of light were sentient, that is exactly what it would experience.

This perception that time may only be a relative reality could account for the strange mystery of quantum entanglement.

Is it also possible that those mystical experiences we encountered earlier, where people have a sense of being at one with the universe and knowing all instantaneously, are because they have somehow shifted perception beyond the perspective of time-bound body-minds? Maybe they do actually see beyond the illusion of space and time.

As Lanza says, "If time is an illusion, if reality is created by our own consciousness, can this consciousness ever be extinguished?".

Fact may yet prove to be even stranger than science fiction and a lot closer to religious mythology than many people suspect.

In India, the myth of Shiva and Shakti sheds a little more light on the interplay of source and matter, which are separate on one level but also indivisible.

Shiva as the timeless, innate, unmoving power behind everything is unknown and inaccessible in deep meditation. It is his union with Shakti—the cosmic energy or female creative power—that brings the world into being.

Through this interplay of consciousness and energy, male and female, light and dark, the universe is created.

Ultimately Shiva and Shakti are not separate but are the transcendent and immanent aspects of the divine.

As Maha Maya, Shakti is the incarnation of the divine energy of the Absolute. Life with all its duality, its extremes of peace and pain, has divinity within it.

Shankara, the father of *Advaita*, wrote a hymn to Shakti (in her form as Lalitha) that says:

> *That which shines within as pure being is her majesty, the supreme empress, absolute consciousness. The universe and all the creatures that range within it are that one reality. Yes, all this is she alone.*

As Ramesh Balsekar expressed it, "The entire manifested creation presents a cosmic dance by the divine dancer, and the dance cannot be differentiated from the dancer."[101]

Krishna in the *Bhagavad Gita* says, "He who sees that the

Lord of all is ever the same in all that is, immortal in the field of mortality—he sees the truth".

Like Christ in the Bible, Krishna speaks from a place of oneness with God. He also includes the manifest universe as inseparable from God, "See now the whole universe with all things that move and move not, and whatever thy soul may yearn to see. See it all as One in me".

It's time for a visit to the Meenakshi Temple, which is a focal point for pilgrims and tourists in Madurai.

The temple is a hugely impressive complex spread over 45 acres. There has been a temple here for millennia but the current building dates from the 17th century. The impressively carved *gopurams* (towers) are visible from most points in the old city, glimpsed along busy streets as you approach and then rising as a grand statement in a splendid technicolour entanglement of gods up close.

Beyond the security gates and shoe-lockers, the temple is a colourful whirlpool of the sacred and the worldly. There are long avenues of columns carved with the images of gods, ceilings painted with vibrantly coloured mandalas, young *brahmin* priests chanting bhajans, stalls with bright knick-knacks and wandering hopefuls selling trinkets. In the midst of it all, sits a huge and very docile, white bull garlanded in marigolds manifesting the spirit of Nandi (Shiva's vehicle). Incense thickens the air, people queue for a glimpse of Meenakshi, groups take photos of each other on cameras and mobile phones, bells ring...

The devout, the curious, the incredulous, beggars, backpackers, families—thousands come each day, as they have for centuries, wearing the stone floors smooth with their bare feet. Many, especially the foreign visitors, are more interested in the splendour and scale than in the ancient myths enacted here but one local custom draws a crowd each evening. It is both timelessly symbolic and touchingly human.

Meenakshi, the goddess of the temple, is a manifestation of Shakti and is Shiva's consort (Meenakshi is the 'fish eyed' goddess—fish eyes being considered very beautiful). As we explored above, Shiva is a symbol of consciousness and Meenakshi is a symbol of energy.

Every night, the priests put Shiva and Meenakshi statues to bed together with much ceremony. Shiva arrives in a musical procession on a silver palanquin, amidst swirls of incense, accompanied by drummers and trumpet players. He is welcomed with garlands of jasmine flowers. Even Meenakshi's nose-stud is removed so she doesn't scratch her lover during their passionate embrace!

They say that if Shiva and Meenakshi are not consummating their union, the universe will come to an end.

20

RELIGION WITHOUT FRONTIERS

CHAMUNDI HILL ON THE OUTSKIRTS of Mysore is 'one of 'South India's eight holiest hills' according to the sign part way up the winding road.

The forecourt of the temple to Chamundi (the local variation of the goddess Durga) is buzzing with pilgrims. There are colourful stalls selling hats, coloured powders and fruit offerings; bangles, brass icons and sandalwood carvings; and the sort of garish toys, teddies and tigers you might find at a fun-fair. There are flowers sellers, persistent wandering postcard sellers and beggars—all hassling for a few rupees.

The melee is similar to how I imagine the scene was at a medieval pilgrimage site such as Canterbury Cathedral. But there are contemporary touches too. The continuous chanting is amplified across the whole area through loud speakers and one stall is selling pictures of gods made of the ridged plastic that makes images appear to move when you tilt it.

"Shiva, Madam? Krishna, Madam? Ganesh, Madam? Buddha, Madam?" asks the enthusiastic young salesman. Here there are no jealous gods. You can take your pick—whoever floats your spiritual boat is fine. Chamundi in her nearby temple is big enough to contain it all—and business is business for the icon salesman!

After paying my respects to Chamundi, I walk back down the 300 steps from the temple to the giant Nandi bull that looks out across Mysore sprawling below on the dry plain. Here on the quiet wooded hillside, the clamour and clatter of the temple forecourt is left behind and it is easier to tune in to the timeless procession of humanity that has worn the steps smooth; to feel the holiness of every leaf and stone.

I pass a well-dressed young woman in a vibrant sari who is marking every stair with *kum kum* as she ascends towards the temple. Her daub of colour adds to the impressionistic pattern of crimson, vermillion and magenta on each step. Her eyes sparkle with joy in what she is doing and I can't help but reflect again that the west has lost something with its inability to bow down and give its heart to something greater.

I wonder too how religions can evolve to be better guides for the sophisticated minds of today—whether they could return to their mystical roots and stop squabbling over doctrine in a way that is losing most people except the fundamentalists who are up for a fight?

Later that day, on the outskirts of Mysore in a quiet suburban station, I visit the 'Vivekananda Express', which has parked up for a few days on its tour of the country to mark the 150th anniversary of Vivekananda's birth.

After narrowly avoiding death as my auto-rickshaw driver decides to take a short-cut the wrong way down a dual-carriageway to get to the entrance, I wander down the station platform in the dusty golden light of late afternoon.

I am one of only half a dozen people here, going from carriage to carriage to view an exhibition of Vivekananda's life and philosophy. Perhaps I am one of the last to get here. I had expected crowds as Vivekananda is one of India's best known and most loved sons, perhaps only second to Gandhi as a revered recent figure.

Outside India, Vivekananda is best known as the charismatic young mystic who made a lasting impression at the Parliament of Religions in Chicago in 1873. His message acknowledged the divinity in all humanity, and the many paths to knowing God. Although he hadn't even planned to be a delegate, his passion and sincerity were acknowledged with two minutes of thunderous applause.

He was also passionate about India and the plight of India's poor—his message that serving the least of humanity is serving Shiva (God) almost paraphrases Christ's instructions. In his relatively short life, he inspired many followers and motivated west and east alike to work to help the poor and dispossessed.

Vivekananda was not someone to accept things on blind faith, least of all the existence of God. Perhaps he was a precursor of many of us in the 20th century and beyond. When he first met his guru, Ramakrishna, he asked him if

Ramakrishna had seen God himself. Ramakrishna replied that he had and this convinced Vivekananda to stay as a disciple.

Vivekananda's path was gruelling, and he suffered from increasingly bad health as a result of it, but what he discovered inspired him to devote his life to teaching and service.

This quote captures his vision of a universal religion. Perhaps our collective despair at the division and fighting between religions, our increasing globalisation and our continuing search for meaning in our lives will lead us to eventually embrace something like this:

> *If there is ever a universal religion, it must be one that will have no location in place or time, one that will be infinite, like the God it will preach; one whose sun will shine upon the followers of Krishna and of Christ, on saints and sinners alike; one that will not be Hindu or Buddhist, Christian or Muslim, Jewish or Jain, but a sum total of all these, with infinite space for development; and one that with its catholicity will embrace in its infinite arms every human being from highest to lowest. It will be a religion that will have no place for persecution or intolerance in its polity, that will recognise divinity in every man and woman, and whose whole scope, whose whole force, will be centred in aiding humanity to realise its own true, divine nature.*[102]

Of course, Vivekananda was not alone in standing against the divisiveness of different creeds.

William James in *Varieties of Religious Experience* said, "I myself invincibly do believe that, although all the special manifestations of religion may have been absurd (I mean its creeds and theories), yet the life of it as a whole is mankind's most important function".[103]

Poet Rumi says:

> *What is to be done, O Muslims for I do not recognise myself,*
> *I am neither a Christian, nor a Jew, nor a Zoroastrian nor a Muslim,*
> *I am not of the East, nor of the West, nor of the land nor of the sea...*
> *My place is Placeless, my Trace is Traceless...*
> *I have rejected duality; I have seen the two worlds as one.*
> *I seek the One, I know the One, I see the One, I call the One.*

Muslim writer Moosa Raza explains how realising the oneness of everything is the key to a more tolerant and encompassing worldview:

> *Once the seer realises the Unity of God—the real spirit of tawhid—and comprehends the concept of the Unity of Mankind—ummatan wahida, as the Qur'an puts it—he can harbour no discrimination in his heart, for he goes beyond the narrow definitions which separate mankind into warring groups based on caste, creed, colour, race and clime.*[104]

Humanity seems to have an innate predisposition to divide. Perhaps this is a left-over from childhood differentiation of objects and the socialisation of behaviour—from 'eating of the tree of knowledge of good and bad'. Or perhaps it was necessary way back in evolution when tribes were our protection.

As well as having within us the capacity for empathy from a very young age, we also have the tendency to divide people into our group and others. By the time children are three years old, they already recognise that people can be divided into different races and genders.

In a parallel of an earlier experiment giving undergraduates red or blue feathers to wear, when three-year-olds were dressed in red or blue T-shirts, they said they would prefer to play with someone of the same colour hair and T-shirt.

In a similar experiment with four- and five-year-olds, the children were arbitrarily dressed in red or blue T-shirts and shown pictures of other children. They tended to judge that others with the same colour T-shirt as them were nicer and that they'd prefer to play with them.[105]

That great predisposition to polarise everything seeps into every aspect of our lives.

The two-party political system in most western societies is a typical example. We seem much better at choosing between two simplistic options than we do to assess an array of non-aligned or complex choices. If we get to the point where three or more parties compete for power, we are in confusion—we want a 'for and against' choice, a proposer and a diametrically opposed opposition.

We want goodies and baddies—we *really* want goodies and baddies—people who share our perspective (good) and people who oppose it (bad).

We put our opposition into a category it's easy to ridicule, dismiss or hate by labelling it and aligning as far as possible away from it. Whether our enemy is greedy capitalists, 'bleeding hearts', tree-hugging greenies, exploitative mining companies, climate-change mongers or climate-change deniers, we like to be clear where we stand and fight our corner.

Media increasingly plays into and inflames this polarity with simplistic reporting of 'for' and 'against' positions. Anyone who has written media releases for ministers knows this dynamic and states a clear position that people can rally behind or align against. There's not much news in sitting on the fence or seeing both sides!

The battle between science and religion is another societal divide that has become polarised, creating division that is encouraged by the media.

Science has become very savvy at promoting its messages, encouraging the publicity that helps win grants and recognition, and enhancing its importance as a thought-leader.

Religion, centuries ago the authority on everything, has slowly lost its grip and finds it hard to gain traction as a credible alternative voice. It is usually stuck with defending a position of belief or moral high-ground that no longer cuts ice or has relevance for much of society.

What's more, it is deserting the ground where it really could offer something of value because most of its spokespeople have not experienced anything of the transcendent. If they have, they struggle to convey it in terms that make sense in a sound-bite or resonate in a materialistic society.

We can't blame religion for religious wars. If those who want to fight over religion had no religion, they would surely still find something to fight over. It could be country boundaries, east-west boundaries, north-south boundaries, racial boundaries, blue-eyed versus brown-eyed boundaries, football team boundaries, haves and have-nots boundaries or belief-in-green-aliens boundaries. Religion may add a layer of self-righteousness to the fight but the battles are started by those who see other views as threatening, feel disenfranchised, insecure or angry.

They also often want to put their energy into a bigger cause to give their life purpose. What is more enticing and meaningful than fighting for God and a reward in heaven?

I feel it's time to move into a new era and see that such divisions are no longer useful for our well-being. To do that, we have to look deeper than our conditioning.

Our different religious texts such as the Koran, the Bible, Buddhist scriptures and the Torah can still have a place. In telling us of our nature in stories and examples of inspirational living beings who have gone before, they are a valuable part of our rich heritage. At their best, they can connect with us at a deeper level than logic alone.

Logical information is processed primarily in the neo cortex, whereas stories involve the insular cortex, which is also involved in processing emotions. Both sides need a role in a balanced human perspective.

Many of these religious stories resonate with mysteries beyond words and provide a catalyst for deeper knowing. In personifying the inexpressible God, they are making it a little easier for people to connect with something transcendent—I don't necessarily mean in prayer or worship designed to achieve merit but perhaps in humility and openness to the miracle we are part of.

Where they lead us astray is where every word is believed literally and where codes of behaviour evolved for other times and places are seen rigidly as intrinsic to holy expression or to reaching heaven.

We can love our religious books and the spirit of their originators without using them to beat others over the head. Ideally, we would see them as facets of the one truth rather than grounds for 'mine is better than yours' arguments.

My search brought me to the conclusion that there is no personal God (or Goddess) monitoring me but the truth is much more profound, mysterious and wondrous. I am part of God as consciousness—never a separate thing except when I believe I am my thoughts, my brain, my body, my history.

The awesome intelligence—the only thing worthy of that fashionable adjective—within everything, and at the same time beyond our limited dimensions, is Perfection beyond human concepts of perfection. It is Love beyond human concepts of love. In quiet moments, we may even know it as bliss.

The mystery of how it was all created and how it all operates may always remain a mystery. It is really not so relevant to spend our time arguing whether there are seven levels of heaven or seven trillion universes. It is a God to be known, not to be measured.

How else can I try to express the inexpressible? God is the consciousness that writes these words and reads these words, attracts atoms together and exuberantly overflows in the life process. It is the life-force that unfolds in myriad ways—whether in the dance of plants unfurling and reaching for the light or in a growing embryo or electrons forming meaningful patterns. Yet this God is so much more than the sum of its biological parts in manifestation.

It matters less what we call this mystery—Allah, Christ, Virgin Mary, Durga, Devi (the Sanskrit root word of 'divine' and the female 'one goddess'), Krishna, Vishnu, Buddha, Achaman, Altjira, Tabaldak, Amaterasu, Great Spirit or the less theistic words like the One, the Source, Cosmic Consciousness, the Totality, Reality, the Absolute—than that we intuit or know it as the ground of what we are.

Could we not acknowledge that we are all trying to talk about the same thing that is beyond words? Could we not become a united voice in standing against science when it attempts to diminish this indescribable essence that makes us all sacred?

For those who have tasted this 'God', it is the only thing that is real in the sense of having a lasting, unchanging reality (beneath and within the changing surface patterns). It is the Truth beyond all fragments of human-perspective truth.

It has the qualities of being, consciousness, bliss, perfection, peace. It is the Love behind love, as the Christians feel. It is the 'clear light' of Buddhist *rigpa*. It is beyond description or form as the Muslims say. It may not have created the world in the literal biblical sense but it is intrinsic to and inseparable from the constantly unfolding creation.

It's not a God who created the world as some past event but one that is part of the creation every moment. It's like a fountain of water that appears to be a solid, constant shaft but it actually fresh droplets all the time. Bohm suggests our senses put together this fountain of being into a solid, much as we hear a sequence of notes as one flow of music or see the many static frames of a movie as continuous action.

Perhaps even atheist Richard Dawkins has felt it when he says in *The God Delusion,* "To sense that behind anything that can be experienced there is a something that our mind cannot grasp and whose beauty and sublimity reaches us only indirectly and as a feeble reflection, this is religiousness. In this sense I am religious".

I disagree with his terminology but not with his sentiment. I don't call what he feels 'religious' because it has little to do with organised religion—it is what those who have explored it more deeply call 'God' and it still needs a place alongside science in humanity's quest for truth.

21

BACK TO THE SOURCE

MORE THAN 35 YEARS after my first visit to Varanasi as a wide-eyed young woman, I am back in this ancient city where the sacred River Ganges draws the Hindu world to purification and prayer, to *darshan* and ultimately to the reality of death.

It has changed less than many other cities in that time. The timescale here seems to be one of millennia rather than decades. The narrow alleys of the old city are still much the same. Tiny one-room shops are still selling all the colourful paraphernalia of Hindu pilgrimage. The river has retreated further down the *ghats* at this time of year, leaving broader expanses of steps where *sadhus* sit, mangy dogs roam and boatmen ply their trade to tourists and pilgrims, but otherwise little has changed.

The sales pressure is stronger than I remember though. I can't walk along the waterfront without the constant cry of 'Boat, boat, Madam, boat!' or 'Come, Madam, finest silks I am showing you!' or 'Come my shop, Madam. Come. Come. Very best price I am giving you!'

A winter haze lies across the water and the sun takes a while to penetrate the muted, misty mornings. Despite the cold, there are dozens of people gathered at dawn on the bathing *ghats,* immersing themselves in the brown water. Women duck under, fully clothed in colourful saris. Men in only a loin cloth clean their teeth, lather their chests or pour handfuls of water over their heads. Mother Ganga is sacred nectar to these people even if she is a polluted torrent to more critical eyes.

Up the river is the main burning *ghat,* Manikarnika. In the years since I was last here, innumerable bodies have been brought to Varanasi's shores. Hundreds are burnt every 24 hours on a fire that is never extinguished and consumes its corpses day and night.

The bodies of men, women and children over the age of five are carried down the adjoining alleyways on pole-stretchers in a constant procession before being lifted onto the pyre. They are covered only by a saffron or orange cloth that conceals their features but not their human shape. (Younger children are considered not to have reached the age of reason and, like holy men and saints, they don't need purification and are buried.)

Families mourn. Generations fall and new ones rise. Life goes on. The procession of bodies never stops.

I know the signs and symbols of this place now. I speak the spiritual language of its people even though I may not agree with every manifestation of its practice. I am part of what they are part of. I'm not only an outsider looking in as I was on my first visit.

Now, in my more mature years, being here beside the burning *ghats* of the Ganges is also a much more poignant reminder that time marches on to a final destination for each of us. However brightly we have burned in life, it is nothing to match the flames or earth that finally consume our physical being.

Is it an ending or a reunion that beckons?

It's easy to understand why humanity in its earliest stages of self-consciousness would have been deeply disturbed on encountering death. Where does this life and consciousness go? Could we arise from nothing and return to nothing? The two book-ends of life are equally mysterious.

I believe the big questions still lurk in all our lives and that death still deeply disturbs us but we have learnt to look the other way. Real death is largely hidden in the west, and fake death on our movie and TV screens has conditioned us to be unshockable—until it touches us or our loved ones.

Most people don't believe there are answers we can know or they hold a hopeful and illogical faith in a heavenly afterlife. They flee deeper into distractions and share well-meaning clichés about life and death, designed to soothe the hollow times of living and the horrific pain of loss.

The disconnection from a real spirituality in our current world seems to me to be one of the greatest challenges facing us.

As the *Vedas* say, "Even if man acquires the capacity to roll up the sky like a piece of leather, there would not be an end to sorrow unless he realises the effulgent one within".

This book alone cannot convince anybody of anything but I hope it will plant a seed for more people to explore our inherent value as human beings and rediscover a sense of sacredness.

I hope it makes the case that the concept of God or a greater intelligence still has a vital role for our balanced lives even if we need to give it a makeover in the light of current science. Most of all, I hope it inspires some others to find their own deeper knowledge of truth with an open mind and an open heart, undeterred by atheist reductionism.

As a society, let's demand more constructive dialogue between science and religion to help our understanding evolve. Let's look for greater dialogue between religions too and less dogma that divides.

Wherever we find wars between religions, it is ignorance, misinterpretation of texts and belief in separateness that drives them. Even Islam, which often gets a bad press these days due to extremists, is fundamentally a religion of unity. The Qor'an says:

> *Argue not with the people of the book except in the fairest manner and say to them 'we believe in what was revealed to us and what was revealed to you. And your God and our God is one and we submit to Him'.*

The Dalai Lama has already initiated a dialogue between science and Buddhism with his 'Mind and Life' conferences and an associated book explains his understanding of where science and Buddhism meet. He says he is willing to adjust Buddhist beliefs where science proves them wrong.

In the concluding chapter he balances his love of science with a caution. "Scientific knowledge, as it stands today, is not complete. Recognising this fact and recognising the limits of scientific knowledge, I believe is essential".[106]

He goes on to say that, without integrating science and the totality of human knowledge, "our conception of the world, including our own existence, will be limited to the facts adduced by science, leading to a deeply reductionist, materialistic, even nihilistic worldview".

In his 1989 Nobel Peace Prize acceptance speech he said:

> *With the ever-growing impact of science on our lives, religion and spirituality have a greater role to play reminding us of our humanity. There is no contradiction between the two. Each gives us valuable insights into the other. Both science and the teaching of the Buddha tell us of the fundamental unity of all things.*

It seems to me that religions should be a stepping stone to experiential discovery and greater understanding not an excuse for a rigid and calcified code of behaviour. They should help people reach their own knowledge, not impose a code of belief.

As Emerson says, "When we have broken our god of tradition, and ceased from our god of rhetoric, then may God fire the heart with his presence".

Einstein doubted whether religion can stretch to contain this broader sweep of a cosmic philosophy, "The religious geniuses of all times have been distinguished by this cosmic religious sense, which recognises neither dogmas nor God made in man's image. Consequently, there cannot be a church whose chief doctrines are based on the cosmic religious experience".[107]

Time will tell whether organised religion will adapt fast enough to meet the emerging knowledge of our era and contain the breadth of vision to see unity rather than division, to inspire knowledge of God rather than ideas about God.

Anthony de Mello—the Jesuit teacher mentioned earlier in this book—quotes former UN Secretary General, Dag Hammarskjöld who said, "God does not die on the day we cease to believe in a personal deity. But we die on the day when our lives cease to be illumined by the steady radiance of wonder renewed daily, the source of which is beyond reason".

Another early morning in Varanasi, I come across some of the men from my hotel huddled around a small street deity. They are wearing beanies against the cold and pouring milk over the faceless impressionistic figure carved in stone in a corner of the alleyway. They chant and make offerings in the shadows where the rising sun has not yet reached.

A little later, when I walk back past them, they are packing up their ritual bowls and leaving. The deity shines from the milk and ghee poured over it. A scrap of cloth adorns it and a few flowers are scattered on the ground. A cow lumbers up, almost filling the width of the alley, and checks if any edibles remain.

I chat with Pandit, a very gentle and humble man who was leading the ritual.

"We have to make the ritual," he says. "When we do not do this, the god loses power."

This seems to me a simple but profound statement of the importance of acknowledging the divine in our lives. As I see it, it is not a distant god that loses power but we who lose the grounding and purpose that comes from knowing a deeper connection with a sacred mystery beyond and within the material world. If it takes the ritual care of a stone deity to reflect our divinity back to us, let's plug into that power. It is there when we bow down, surrender ourselves and honour our God in whatever way speaks to us.

Perhaps then we will see with the eyes of Kabir, a son of Varanasi who lived in the 15th century and is revered by Hindus and Muslims alike:

> *But that formless God takes a thousand forms in the eyes of His creatures:*
> *He is pure and indestructible,*
> *His form is infinite and fathomless*
> *He dances in rapture and waves of form arise from His dance*
> *The body and mind cannot contain themselves when they are touched by His great joy.*
> *He is immersed in all consciousness, all joys, and all sorrow;*
> *He has no beginning and no end;*
> *He holds all within His bliss.*[108]

Sitting on the guesthouse terrace, high above the Ganges,

where children fly simple home-made kites from the rooftops and monkeys shriek in the trees, the personal life seems so insignificant in its brief flowering. Yet each of us is the visible face of God smiling. Each of us is the heart of God loving. Each of us is the mystery of God in motion.

Somewhere beyond time, I'm still here in Varanasi as a young woman with Jake. I'm still a child playing with my sister on the cool, wet sand of an English beach while our parents look on. I'm sharing a cigarette with Lesley, the school friend who made teen years bearable. I'm sitting close to my college friend John as clouds scurry across the Sussex Downs and we discuss life and love. I'm walking arm-in-arm with Ellis in the summer moonlight in Kent and climbing a hillside through sparkling, thick snow, treading in his footprints. I'm high on Mahabeleshewar mountain looking out at infinity as dusty sunset turns to dusk and dogs bark way below. I'm baking cakes with Atosh for a *sannyasin* celebration. I'm holding my sweet baby daughter in my arms for the first time.

I'm waking with Chandragiri in a bamboo hut on a Mexican beach as dawn breaks through the slats. I'm watching my daughter grow through the days of school books and colourful parrots in the garden. I'm listening to Sam play beautiful guitar and seeing him smile. I'm flowing with love and motion on the back of Jamie's motorbike. I'm standing with my sister at my dying father's bedside and sitting with her on a roof-terrace in Morocco. I'm on my deck in Australia listening to the magpies while bees and butterflies makes patterns in the sunshine.

I'm swimming in the Mediterranean, the Aegean, and the Caribbean seas; the Pacific and the Indian oceans. I'm walking on beaches and pavements and mountains. I'm laughing, I'm crying, I'm confused, I'm lonely, I'm meditating, I'm writing, I'm dancing, I'm making love, I'm sitting at the feet of gurus. I'm taking my last breath at a place as yet unknown.

I am in a thousand million moments of this amazing, incredible life where I travelled in search of God. How could it be otherwise?

I'll leave Vivekananda to sum it up in words that ring true across more than a century.

> *After long searches here and there, in temples and in churches, in earths and in heavens, at last you come back, completing the circle from where you started, to your own soul and find that He for whom you have been seeking all over the world, for whom you have been weeping and praying in churches and temples, on whom you were looking as the mystery of all mysteries shrouded in the clouds, is nearest of the near, is your own Self, the reality of your life, body, and soul...*

EPILOGUE

ON THE FLOOD PLAIN OF THE GANGES and the Yamuna rivers in Allahabad, once every 12 years when the planetary aspects are right, millions of people converge for not only the biggest religious festival on earth, but the biggest event on earth.

A city of tents and infrastructure grows from nothing in the short two months or so after the monsoon river recedes—streets, ashrams galore, lighting, electricity, sanitation, sound systems, pontoon bridges, hospitals, police stations and a huge security force.

Leaving footprints on sandy dust, around 100 million people over a few weeks (and up to 30 million on auspicious days) came to the sacred *sangam* of the Ganges, Yamuna and invisible Saraswati river to bathe, believing that the water is 'nectar' at this time.

The people who come are not only *sadhus* and simple folk, but Indians from every walk of life—doctors from Delhi, lawyers and stockbrokers from Mumbai, engineers from Bangalore, students, teachers and university professors.

The 2013 event was the Maha Kumbh Mela—the great Kumbh Mela, which happens once every 144 years.

Here, every street offers a smorgasbord of holy men behind instant medieval-looking fortifications, temporary temple archways, bright flourishes of disposable architecture, flashing lights and tinsel. It's almost Las Vegas, with billboards showing super-sized smiling men (and a few women) in white or orange robes instead of cabaret stars. At this festival, gurus rule and there are hundreds of them to choose from, most never heard of outside India.

There are stalls selling all sorts of religious paraphernalia—flowers for *aarti,* coloured powders, *rudraksha* beads—plus wandering vendors with colourful whirly-gigs for the children, peacock feather fans for the ladies and carts of peanuts, sesame sweets or fried snacks for hungry pilgrims.

The stars of the show are the tens of thousands of *sadhus*—renunciates who wander the country or live around temples—from different sects in different shades of saffron or fiery orange. Each group congregates in a tent town beneath a coloured flag.

I visit one of their tents with my Indian guide.

It's a bit like going to a bizarre ancient court. The chief secretary greets us and orders young *sadhus* to bring chai. A chillum is also offered. Then the chief baba appears from deeper in the tented palace to hold audience. I can't follow the conversation but there seems to be both relaxed banter and reverence. I think there's some sort of deal going down too. Calls are made by mobile phone. Other *sadhus* are consulted. Business cards are swapped. Twenty minutes later we emerge into the light with *namastes* all round.

I smile at the modified renunciation, which allows all these contemporary tools, at least for the senior members!

Although some of the *sadhus* are undoubtedly impressive with their dreadlocks and deep eyes that seem to see infinity and glow with eternal contentment, there are as many who look like a ragged band of misfits who have got together to live with the support of a wandering gentlemen's club.

Some of the more extreme *sadhus* demonstrate their disregard of body and their single-focus on God through painful austerities. They stand on display, almost like circus freaks but revered by those who gawk.

One has stood for decades, with one arm raised above his head, supported by a sling while he sleeps vertically. Another *sadhu* stands on one leg as he has for many years. Another has a bundle of bricks constantly attached to his penis, which has stretched and become useless as a sexual organ.

It's strange how both these *sadhus* and some earlier Christian saints find it necessary to mortify the body. As if life doesn't present enough pain and challenges without doing such dire things to the wonder of the living body!

This seems to demonstrate the extremes of the dualistic worldview that divides good and evil, spirit and body, God and sinning humankind.

The *naga babas* are the famous, dreadlocked, ash-smeared Shiva *sadhus* wearing nothing but *rudraksha* beads. In a hierarchical arrangement, they lead the *arkhara* (particular sects or regiments of *sadhus*) into the river on bathing days. They are the stars of the most iconic photos of the festival, beamed around the world by TV and internet.

Walking the dusty river-bed streets that cover about 50 square kilometres, I feel the palpable excitement of being part of the largest spiritual gathering on earth and one whose history goes back thousands of years. While the earliest written records of Chinese travellers observing the event date from the 7th century CE, it is widely accepted that its origins precede this by centuries, possibly by millennia.

Most of the time, the atmosphere is nothing like the quiet reverence I used to associate with spirituality but more like a rock festival, carnival or the Australian agricultural shows, which are an extravaganza of family fun, fairground rides, amplified announcements and dubious food traditions.

I am camping in relatively civilised tourist tents about five kilometres away from the *mela* ground itself.

Tomorrow is one of the major bathing days and, as I hunker down under piles of blankets on a near-freezing, crisp, dry night, the crowd noise and music are a constant hum reaching through the still darkness.

As the night progresses, the crowd rumble grows—hundreds of different chants amplified from thousands of loudspeakers around the *mela* ground. Multitudes are praising God—'*Om Namah Shivayah, Ram Jai Ram, Hare Krishna*'. Conch shells and trumpets are bellowing like cattle in pain. '*Om Namah Shivayah, Ram Jai Ram, Hare Krishna*.' It is a strange other-worldly sound that stays on the edge of my consciousness through restless sleep.

Then, as dawn approaches, it reaches a roaring crescendo, a thunderous cacophony of chanting and instruments—millions of souls reaching out to God.

Suddenly it no longer seems an amazing spiritual phenomenon but the terrible sound of hell. It's the anguished sound of yearning and separation, the sound of humanity clamouring for something just beyond reach.

At that moment, I am also aware of the infinitely deep stillness of knowing God within, the certainty of that presence being accessible wherever I am. I am *Devi,* the totality, the ultimate reality. I am That. I am the life, love and consciousness that pervades all.

For maybe an hour the Julia-self dissolves in that state of perfect peace. No need for church. No need for the temple. No need for gurus. No need for bathing in sacred rivers or making pilgrimages. No need to even name or conceptualise God.

A little later that morning, I set out again to witness the incredible colour, community and rituals of the Kumbh Mela—the amazing spectacle and timeless tradition of people searching for something infinitely valuable that is always present, if only we are still enough to realise it.

✦

EXPLANATION OF INDIAN/SANSKRIT TERMS

aarti – a Hindu ritual offering of fire to a god or goddess
Advaita Vedanta – Advaita is literally 'not two', and Vedanta refers to the different paths of Hindu philosophy. Advaita Vedanta is a non-dual philosophy dating back to the Vedas.
akhara – literally 'a place of practice'. Groups of sadhus belong to an *akhara*.
atman – the individual soul or living essence
Bhagavad Gita – literally 'Song of the Lord', this is one of the central texts in the Hindu tradition. Much of it is a dialogue between God incarnate Krishna and Arjuna, a warrior. Thought to date to around 400 BCE and 200 CE. There are many translations and interpretations. I recommend the Penguin Classic with translation by Juan Mascaro.
Brahma – one of the three main gods in the Hindu trinity. Vishnu and Shiva are the other two.
Brahman – the Absolute or Supreme cosmic principle
brahmin – a priest of Hinduism, part of the *brahmin* caste of priests and teachers
charpoy – a traditional bed consisting of a wooden frame with rope or woven base
darshan – literally a 'glimpse' or 'view', applied to seeing a deity or a blessing given by a guru
Devi – the female goddess or the divine female. In Hinduism she is personified in the various female goddesses including Durga, Parvati, Saraswathi and Laxmi.
Durga – one of the female forms of the goddess – often seen with a

tiger, she is a warrior goddess.
Ganesh – the popular elephant-headed Hindu god – son of Shiva and Parvati
ghat – step down to the river, especially the wide steps on the river bank that may be used for bathing, laundry or religious ceremonies
guru – literally 'teacher' but most often used for a religious teacher. The Sanskrit root gu means darkness or ignorance, and ru denotes the remover of that darkness.
*Guru Purnim*a – a traditional festival when disciples honour the guru – held at full moon in June/July
Krishna – an incarnation of the god Vishnu and a supreme god in his own right. He is the central teaching character in the Bhagavad Gita.
Kumbh Mela – an ancient religious festival of pilgrimage held once every 12 years at Allahabad in north India at the confluence of sacred rivers. It is the largest gathering of humanity for an event. Smaller melas are held every three years at other holy cities. The Maha Kumbh Mela is every 144 years and was held in 2013.
kum kum – powder made from turmeric or other coloured sources, used in religious ceremonies and to mark the forehead at the third eye
lila – loosely translated as 'play', it is a Sanskrit term applied to the spontaneous manifestation of Brahman
maya – the illusion that the phenomenal world is real or ignorance of the reality of self
Maha Maya – the goddess who destroys illusions or the divinity within the illusion
mala – a string of beads used in meditation, sometimes with a picture of the guru
mela – festival
namaste – Indian greeting with hands folded, acknowledges the divine in each person
Nandi – the sacred bull, Shiva's vehicle, often seen outside temples in India
naga babas – naked sadhus, renunciates
Nataraja – literally 'king of dancers' applied to Shiva as the cosmic dancer whose dance is creation
Qur'an (Koran) – Islamic holy book

rigpa – pure awareness, the natural state of the mind
rudraksha – the seeds from the rudraksha tree are often used in malas. The word translates as 'Shiva's eye'.
Sabarimala – a south Indian festival
sadhu – a religious ascetic, monk or any holy person in Hinduism and Jainism who has renounced the worldly life
samadhi – a merging with the Absolute, usually achieved in meditation. Maha samadhi ('great samadhi' is consciously merging with the Absolute at the death of the body.
sangam – a confluence of rivers, especially that of the Ganges, Yamuna and Saraswathi at Allahabad
sannyasin – one who has renounced material things. Rajneesh's neo-sannyasins were initiated disciples who wore orange and a mala.
satchitananda – being-consciousness-bliss – the ultimate unchanging reality and characteristic of Brahman
satsang – being with the truth, often used for a gathering with the guru
Shankara – also called Shankaracharya, a philosopher thought to have been born around 750 CE. He is considered to be the founding father of Advaita Vedanta but is clear the concepts precede him by many centuries. His flair for debating and teaching helped cement the philosophy in India.
Shiva – one of the gods of the Hindu trinity and a personification of Brahman. Brahma and Vishnu are the other two in the trinity.
Sufi – an Islamic mystic.
Vedas – a collection of hymns and other ancient religious texts written in India between about 1500 and 1000 BCE.
Vishnu – one of the three main gods in the Hindu trinity. Shiva and Brahma are the other two.

BIBLIOGRAPHY

Almaas, A.H. *Facets of Unity*. Berkeley: Diamond Books, 1998.

—. *Luninous Night's Journey*. Berkeley: Diamond Books, 1995.

Anonymous. *The Penny Catchism*. USA: Tan Books & Publishers Inc, 2009 (reprinted).

Armstrong, Karen. *The Case for God*. New York: Anchor Books, 2010.

Attar, Farrid Al-Din. *Muslim Saints and Mystics*. London: Arkana, 1990.

Baggini, Julian. *The Ego Trick*. London: Granta Books, 2011.

Balsekar, Ramesh S. *Confusion No More*. Mumbai: Zen Publications, 2003.

—. *The Final Truth*. Redondo Beach: Advaita Press, 1989.

Basham, A. L. *The Wonder That Was India*. New York: Grove Press, 1954.

Beauregaard, Mario and O'Leary, Denise. *The Spiritual Brain*. New York: Harper & Collins, 2008.

Bhaunik, Mani. *Code Name God*. New Delhi: Penguin, 2005.

Bohm, David. *Wholeness and the Implicate Order*. Oxford: Routledge & Kegan Paul, 1980.

Campbell, Joseph. *The Hero with a Thousand Faces*. London: Fontana Press, 1993.

Capra, Fritjof. *The Tao of Physics*. Boulder: Shambala Publications, 1975.

Caprice, Alice. *The New Quotable Einstein*. Princeton: Princeton University Press, 2005.

Chalmers, David. *The Character of Consciousness*. New York: Oxford University Press, 2010.

Coburn, Thomas B. *Encountering the Goddess*. New York: State University of New York Press, 1991.

Cohen, S. S. *Guru Ramana*. Tiruvannamalai: Sri Ramanasramamam, 1980.

Cole-Adams. *Anaesthesia*. Melbourne: Text Publishing Company, 2017.

Crick, Francis and Koch, Christof. "A Framework of Consciousness." *Nature Neuroscience* (2003).

Damasio, Antonio. *Self Comes to Mind*. New York: Vintage Books, 2012.

Davies, Paul. *Superforce*. London: Heinemann, 1984.

Dawkins, Richard. *The God Delusion*. London: Black Swan, 2007.

de Botton, Alain. *Relgion for Atheists: A Non-believer's Guide to the Uses of Religion*. London: Pnguin Books, 2014.

De Mello, Anthony. *Awareness*. New York: Doubleday, 1990.

—. *Awareness*. Harper & Collins, 1990.

DeLuca, Dave. *Pathways to Joy - The Master Vivekananda*. Hawaii: Inner Ocean Publishing, 2006.

Dossey, Larry. *One Mind*. New York: Hay House, 2013.

Du Boulay, Shirley. *The Cave of the Heart*. New York: Orbis Books, 2005.

Eck, Diana L. *India: A Sacred Geography*. New York: Harmony Books, 2012.

Ehrenreich, Barbara. *Living with a Wild God*. London: Granta, 2014.

Einstein. *Einstein On Cosmic Religion and Other Aphorisms*. New York: Dover Publications, 2009.

Eliade, Mircia. *From Primitives to Zen*. Fount Paperbacks, 1977.

Elwes, R. H. M. *The Chief Works of Benedict de Spinoza*. Michagan: G. Bell, 1887.

Emerson, Ralph Waldo. *Reliance & Other Essays*. Dover, 1993.

Everett, Daniel. *Don't Sleep There Are Snakes*. USA: Random House, 2009.

Flanagan, Owen. *The Really Hard Problem—Meaning in a Material World*. Cambridge: Massachusets University of Technology Press, 2009.

Fox, Matthew. *Meditations with Meister Eckhardt*. Santa Fe: Bear & Company, 1983.

Freke, Timothy. *The Wisdom of Sufi Sages*. Boston: Godsfield Press, 1998.

—. *Wisdom of the Christian Mystics*. Boston: Godsfield Press, 1998.

Glucklich, Ariel. *Climbing Chamundi Hill*. London: Bantam, 2004.

Gopnik, Alison. *The Philosophical Baby*. New York: Picador, 2009.

Goswami, Amit. *God Is Not Dead*. Mumbai: Jaico Publishing House, 2009.

—. *The Self Aware Universe*. London: Simon & Schuster, 1993.

Greene, Brian. *The Elegant Universe*. USA: W.W. Norton, 2003.

Happold, F.C. *Mysticism*. London: Penguin, 1963.

Hawking, Stephen and Mlodinow, Leonard. *The Grand Design*. London: Bantam Books, 2010.

Hitchens, Christopher. *God is Not Great: How Religions Poison Everything*. London: Atlantic Books, 2008.

Hood, Bruce. *The Self Illusion*. London: Constable & Robinson, 2011.

Hoskote, Ranjit (Translator). *I, Lalla*. New Delhi: Penguine Books India, 2011.

I., Gurdjieff G. *Views from the Real World*. London: Routledge & Kegan Paul, 1976.

Krishnamurti, J. *Commentaries on Living (Second Series)*. London: Victor Gollanz, 1986.

James, William. *The Varieties of Religious Experience*. New York: Penguin, 1982.

Kahneman, Daniel. *Thinking Fast and Slow*. London: Penguin Books, 2012.

Kauffman, Stuart A. *Reinventing the Sacred*. New York: Basic Books, 2010.

Khan, Hazrat Inayat. *The Purpose of Life*. London: The Sufi Movement, 1927.

Kornfield, Jack. *After the Ecstasy, the Laundry*. London: Rider, 2000.

Lama, Dalai. *Dzogchen*. Boston: Snow Lion, 2000.

—. *The Universe in a Single Atom*. New York: Three Rivers Press, 2005.

Lanza, Robert. *Biocentrism*. Dallas: BenBella, 2009.

Laszlo, Ervin. *The Immortal Mind*. Rochester: Inner Traditions, 2014.

Lederman, Leon M & Hill Christopher T. *Quantum Physics for Poets*. New York: Prometheus Books, 2011.

Lipton, Bruce H. *The Biology of Belief*. USA: Hay House, 2005.

Long, Barry. *Knowing Yourself*. London: The Barry Long Foundation, 1983.

—. *My Life of Love and Truth*. Barry Long Foundation, 2013.

—. *Only Fear Dies*. London: Barry Long Books, 1996.

—. *Wisdom and Where To Find It*. London: Barry Long Foundation, 1994.

Longchempa (translation Lipman, K and Peterson, M). *You Are the Eyes of the World*. New York: Snpw Lion Publications, 2000.

Maharaj, Nisargadatta. *Beyond Freedom*. Mumbai: Yogi Impressions, 2007.

—. *I am That*. Mumbai: Chetana Press, 1973.

—. *The Experience of Nothingness*. Berkeley: Atlantic Books, 1996.

Mahler, Margaret S. *The Psychological Birth of the Human Infant*. London: Routledge, 1975.

Mascaro, Juan (Translator). *The Bhagavad Gita*. London: Penguin, 1962.

Mascaro, Juan. *The Upanishads*. London: Penguin , 1965.

McCarthy, S. J. (translator). *Al-Ghazali's Path to Sufism*. Louisville: Fons Vitae, 2000.

McGilchrist, Ian. *The Master and his Emissary*. London: Yale University Press, 2009.

McGinn. *The Mysterious Flame*. Ingram Publisher Services, 2000.

Menon, Y Keshava. *The Mind of Adi Shankaracharya*. Mumbai: Jaico, 2011.

Merton, Thomas. *Seeds of Contemplation*. Wheathampstead: Anthony Clarke Books, 1972.

Metzinger, Thomas. *The Ego Tunnel*. New York: Basic Books, 2009.

Muktananda, Swami. *Nothing Exists That Is Not Shiva*. Ganeshpuri: SYDA Foundation, 1997.

Naars, Bernard J. *In the Theatre of Consciousness*. Oxford: Oxford University Press, 1997.

Nikhilananda, Swami. *Vivekananda, A biogrpahy*. Calcutta: Advaita Ashrama, 2001.

Osborne, Arthur. *For Those with Little Dust: Pointers on the Teachings of Ramana Maharshi*. Carlsbad: Inner Directions Publishing, 2001.

Peat, David F. *Infinite Potential. The Life and Times of David Bohm*. New York: Basic Books, 1996.

Penrose, Roger. *Shadows of the Mind*. London: Vintage, 2005.

Perry, J & Bratman M. *Introduction to Philosophy*. Oxford: Oxford University Press, 1999.

Probram, Karl H. *The Form Within*. USA: Prospecta Press, 2013.

Rajneesh, Bhagwan Shree. *The Imprisoned Splendour*. Poona: Rajneesh Foundation, 1979.

Raza, Moosa. *In Search of Oneness*. New Delhi: Penguin Ananda, 2012.

Reanney, Darryl. *Death of Forever*. Melbourne: Longman Cheshire, 1991.

—. *Music of the Mind*. Melbourne: Hill of Content, 1994.

Ropp, Robert De. *The Master Game*. London: Picador, 1974.

Sacks, Jonathan. *The Great Partnership*. London: Hodder & Stoughton, 2011.

Schrodinger, Erwin. *What is Life (With Mind and Matter)*. Cambridge:

Cambridge University Press, 2012.
Selbie, Joseph. *The Physics of God.* New Jersey: The Career Press, 2018.
Serrano, Miguel. *The Serpent of Paradise, The Story of an Indian Pilgrimage.* London: Routledge, Kegan & Paul, 1974.
Sorl, Wolf-Dieter. *Shiva, The Wild God of Power and Ecstacy.* Rochester: Inner Traditions, 2004.
Sunyata. *Dancing with the Void.* New Delhi: New Age Books, 2004.
Tagore, Rabinranath. *Gitanjali.* New York: Scibner Poetry, 1997.
—. *Songs of Kabir.* Digireads.com, 2011.
Talbot, Michael. *The Holographic Universe.* New York: Harper Collins, 1991.
Tallis, Raymond. *Aping Mankind.* Acumen, 2011.
—. *The Kingdom of Infinite Space.* London: Atlantic Books, 2008.
Taylor, Jill Bolte. *My Stroke of Insight.* London: Hodder & Stoughton, 2008.
Tolle, Eckhardt. *The Power of Now.* London: Hodder and Stoughton, 2001.
Traditional. *Ashtavakra Gita, Special edition.* Tiruvannamalai: Sri Ramanashramam, 2001.
Trungpa, Chogyam. *Cutting Through Spiritual Materialism.* Boston: Shambala, 2002.
Tweedie, Irina. *Daughter of Fire.* Nevada: Blue Dolphin Press, 1986.
Underhill, Evelyn. *Mysticism.* New York: E.P. Dutton, 1930.
Vanamali. *Shakti. Realm of the Divine Mother.* Vermont: Inner Traditions, 2006.
Webb, Jeremy. *Nothing.* London: Profile Books, 2013.
Women, Gay'Wu Group of. *Song Spirals.* Sydney: Allen & Unwin, 2019.

REFERENCES

1 http://www.guardian.co.uk/media/2004/aug/10/pressandpublishing.guardianobituaries

2 *King James Bible,* Matthew 8:22

3 *Scriptures in Silence and Sermons in Stone,* Bhagwan Shree Rajneesh, Rajneesh Foundation, 1979

4 Source lost – from my early notes

5 *The Imprisoned Splendour,* Bhagwan Shree Rajneesh, Rajneesh Foundation, 1978

6 *Ancient Music in the Pines,* Bhagwan Shree Rajneesh, Rajneesh Foundation, 1977

7 *Scriptures in Silence and Sermons in Stone,* Bhagwan Shree Rajneesh, Rajneesh Foundation, 1979

8 *Knowing Yourself,* Barry Long, Barry Long Foundation, 1983

9 *'Love is not a feeling'.* Article in 'What is Enlightenment?', Volume 4, Number 2, 1995

10 http://www.barrylong.org/statements/life as-it-is.shtml

11 *Mysticism* Evelyn Underhill, Digireads Publishing 2005 (original edition 1910)

12 *The Upanishads,* Juan Mascaro, Penguin, 1965

13 *Guru Ramana,* S.S. Cohen, Sri Ramanasramam, 1980

14 *Awareness,* Anthony de Mello, Doubleday, 1990

15 *Cutting Through Spiritual Materialism,* Shambala, 1973

16 *The Psychological Birth of the Human Infant,* Margaret Mahler, Routledge, 1975

20 *The Varieties of Religious Experience,* William James, Penguin, 1982

21 *Code Name God,* Mani Bhaunik, Penguin India, 2005

22 *The Power of Now,* Eckhart Tolle, Hodder & Stoughton, 2001

23 *My Life of Love and Truth,* Barry Long Foundation International, 2013

24 Interview with the author

25 *Living with a Wild God,* Granta Publications, 2014

26 *Daughter of Fire,* Irina Tweedie, Blue Dolphin Press, 1986

27 *Anaesthesia,* Kate Cole-Adams, Text Publishing Company, 2017

28 *In the Theater of Consciousness,* Bernard J Naars, Oxford University Press 1997

29 *A framework of consciousness,* Francis Crick and Christof Koch, Nature Neuroscience, February 2003

30 *The Self Illusion,* Bruce Hood, Constable & Robinson, 2011

31 *Self Comes to Mind,* Antonio Damasio, Vintage Books, 2012

32 *Aping Mankind,* Raymond Tallis, Acumen, 2011

33 *The Spiritual Brain,* Mario Beauregard, Harper One, 2008

34 *Biocentrism,* Robert Lanza, Ben Bella Books, 2009

35 *Shadows of the Mind,* Roger Penrose, Vintage Books, 2005

36 *Song Spirals,* Gay'Wu Group of Women, Allen & Unwin, NSW 2019

37 German sermon 4 http://www.eckhartsociety.org/resources/eckhart-and-related-resources-line accessed 06.05.2013

38 *The Wisdom of the Christian Mystics,* Timothy Freke, Godsfield Press, 1998

39 *The Wisdom of the Sufi Sages,* Timothy Freke, Godsfield Press, 1998

40 *The Bhagavad Gita* Penguin Classics, translation Juan Mascaro, 1962

41 *The Spiritual Brain,* Mario Beauregard, Harper One, 2008

42 Interview with the author

43 Interview with the author

44 http://www.newscientist.com/article/dn9522/magic-mushrooms-really-cause-spiritual-experiences.html#.Uo06j8S7dGY accessed 21.11.2013

45 *Dancing with the Void,* Sunyata, Blue Dove Press, 2001

46 *Krishnamurti Commentaries on Living - Second Series* Gollancz, 1990

47 *The Wonder That Was India,* Translation A.L. Basham, 1954

49 From the *Book of Overthrowing Apophis,* quoted by Mircia Eliade in *From Primitives to Zen,* Fount Paperbacks 1977

50 *India, A Sacred Geography,* Diana L Eck, Harmony Books, 2012

51 *Encountering the Goddess,* Thomas B Coburn, State University of New York Press, 1991

52 *The Hero with a Thousand Faces,* Joseph Campbell, Fontana Press, 1993

53 *Biocentrism*, Robert Lanza, BenBella, 2009

54 *The Elegant Universe*, Brian Greene, W. W. Norton, 2003

55 http://www.scientificamerican.com/article/according-to-the-big-bang/ Accessed 13.02.2014

56 *Shiva the Wild God of Power and Ecstasy*, Wold-Dieter Storl, Inner Traditions, 2004

57 http://www.fritjofcapra.net/shiva.html Accessed 11.09.2013

58 *Bhagavad Gita*, Juan Mascaro (Translator), Penguin Books, 1962

59 *Luminous Night's Journey*, A. H. Almaas, Diamond Books, 1995

60 *The Wisdom of Hindu Gurus*, Timothy Freke, Journey Editions, 1998

61 *Superforce*, Paul Davies, Heinemann, 1984

62 *Music of the Mind*, Darryl Reanney,Hill of Content, 1994

63 *The Wisdom of Christian Mystics*, Timothy Freke, Journey Editions, 1998

64 *The Wisdom of Hindu Gurus*, Timothy Freke, Journey Editions, 1998

65 *Ashtavakra Gita*, Special edition, Sri Ramanashramam, 2001

66 *The Chief Works of Benedict de Spinoza*, R.H.M. Elwes, G. Bell, 1887

67 *The Character of Consciousness*, David Chalmers, Oxford University Press, 2010

68 *Reinventing the Sacred*, Stuart A Kauffman, Basic Books New York 2010

69 *Wholeness and the Implicate Order*, David Bohm, Routledge & Kegan Paul, 1980

70 *Gitanjali*, Rabindranath Tagore, MacMillan Publishing Company, 1913

71 *Cutting through Spiritual Materialism*, Chögyam Trungpa *Cutting Through Spiritual Materialism*, Shambala 1973

72 *Don't Sleep There Are Snakes*, Daniel Everett, Random House, 2009

73 *King James Bible*; Genesis 3

74 *The New Quotable Einstein*, Alice Calaprice, Princeton University Press, 2005

75 *Introduction to Philosophy*, Edited John Perry and Michael Bratman, Oxford University Press, 1999

76 *Gitanjali*, Rabindranath Tagore, MacMillan Publishing Company, 1913

77 *King James Bible*, Matthew 13:55

78 *The Purpose of Life*, Hazrat Inayat Khan, The Sufi Movement, 1927

79 *I, Lalla*, Penguin Books India, 2011

80 *Reliance and Other Essays* Ralph Waldo Emerson, Dover edition 1993 (first

published Boston 1841)

81 *Confusion No More,* Ramesh Balsekar, 2003

82 *Facets of Unity,* A. H. Almaas, Diamond Books, 1998

83 *King James Bible,* Matthew 6:26

84 *What is Life?* With *Mind and Matter,* Cambridge University Press, 1967

85 *Facets of Unity,* A. H. Almaas, Diamond Books, 1998

86 *Visuddimagga,* (Path of Purification) traditional Buddhist text, 5th century CE

87 *Confusion No More,* Ramesh Balsekar, Zen Publications, 2003

88 *The Case for God,* Karen Armstrong, Anchor Books, 2010

89 *The Master and His Emissary,* Ian McGilchrist, Yale University Press, 2009

90 *The God Delusion,* Richard Dawkins, Black Swan, 2007

91 *God is Not Great: How Religions Poison Everything,* Christopher Hitchens, Atlantic books, 2008

92 Colin Blakemore, *The Observer,* 22 February 2009

93 *The Really Hard Problem. Meaning in a Material World,* Owen Flanagan, Massachusetts Institute of Technology Press, 2009

94 From *Radical Philosophy,* reproduced in *Introduction to Philosophy,* edited by John Perry, Michael Bratman, Oxford University Press, 1999

95 *God is Not Dead,* Amit Goswami, Jaico Publishing, 2009

96 https://www.sciencemag.org/news/2017/06/china-s-quantum-satellite-achieves-spooky-action-record-distance

97 *The Form Within,* Karl H. Pribram, Prospecta Press, 2013

98 *My Stroke of Insight,* Jill Bolte Taylor, Hodder & Stoughton, 2008

99 *One Mind,* Larry Dossey, MD, Hay House, 2013

100 *Wholeness and the Implicate Order,* David Bohm, Routledge & Kegan Paul, 1980

101 *The Final Truth,* Ramesh Balsekar, Advaita Press, 1989

102 *Pathways to Joy - the Master Vivekananda* Edited Dave DeLuca, Inner Ocean Publishing, 2006

103 *The Varieties of Religious Experience,* William James, Penguin, 1982

104 In *Search of Oneness,* Moosa Raza Penguin Ananda, 2012

105 *The Philosophical Baby,* Alison Gopnik, Picador, 2009

106 *The Universe in a Single Atom,* Dalai Lama, Three Rivers Press, 2005

107 *Einstein on Cosmic Religion and Other Opinions & Aphorisms*, Dover Publications, 2009, original 1931

108 *Songs of Kabir*, translated by Rabindranath Tagore, Digireads.com Publishing, 2011